D1637001

An Encyclopedia of KNIVES

Other Books by the Author

The Hunter's Almanac
The Fisherman's Almanac (with Dan Morris)
Family Fun Around the Water (with Dan Morris)
Camping in Comfort (with Sil Strung)
Spinfishing (with Milt Rosko)
Deer Hunting
Whitewater! (with Sam Curtis and Earl Perry)
Misty Mornings and Moonless Nights
Communicating the Outdoor Experience (editor)

An Encyclopedia of KNIVES
by Norman Strung

Line drawings by C. W. "Wally" Hansen
Photographs by the author

J. B. Lippincott Company
Philadelphia & New York

Copyright © 1976 by Norman Strung
All rights reserved
First edition

Printed in the United States of America

U.S. Library of Congress Cataloging in Publication Data

Strung, Norman.
    An encyclopedia of knives.

    1. Knives.   I. Title.
TS380.S74   621.9'3   76–10288
ISBN–0–397–01164–4

To my father, who bought me my first knife.
To my mother, who was sure I'd cut myself
(she was right).

Contents

Foreword

As I BEGIN MY FINAL DRAFT OF THIS, my tenth book, I am no less amazed at public reaction to its subject matter than I was when it was a germ of an idea. "A book about knives? How could you ever write a whole book about knives?" most people ask me in disbelief.

In that question lies the very reason for my interest in, and enthusiasm for, the subject. Conservatively, there are at least a thousand different kinds of knives with different combinations of blade design, edge, steel, and handles and, more important, different functions. Few people realize this; to them, a knife is a knife. To consider all knives by the same set of criteria, however, would be like adding grapefruit and apples.

In fact, a knife is a tool, and each minute difference in design denotes a different kind of tool with a different use. Carving meat with a bread knife is a little like hammering a nail with a wrench: it gets the job done, but there's a much better way. It's also interesting to note that everyone reading this will immediately know the difference between a hammer and a wrench, but I'd be surprised if one out of ten could tell the difference between a carver and a bread knife.

My interest in the subject is also more than academic. I have used knives all my life, and a wider variety than most people have used at that. As an avid sportsman, I have carried knives hunting, fishing, and camping from the Arctic to the Equator. Cooking, another hobby of mine, sometimes entails my butchering the big game my wife and I shoot as well as the livestock we raise. In addition, woodworking and gardening are more than hobbies to both of us. We raise our own fruits

9

and vegetables for home consumption, and we built our home and out-buildings in Montana with our own hands—and our own cutting tools.

Somewhere during that long and broad association with knives, I began to perceive the economy of motion and excellence of result that are achieved by using the right cutting edge for the job and by using the tool correctly. Coupled with the undeniable facts that every one of us comes in contact with knives at some point in our day and that few of us understand these tools, my perception grew into an idea, and that idea grew into this book.

So, while I'm continually amazed that people question the need for a book about knives, I'm not at all disturbed. So long as I hear "a knife is a knife," there will be a need.

Acknowledgments

Special thanks to Bob Farquharson of the Case Cutlery Company and Bob Stamp of the Queen Cutlery Company for their time, opinions, and advice on the preparation of this manuscript; to Bruce Pitcher for darkroom technique that lifted many of my photos from the prosaic to the sublime; to Wally Hansen for his exacting hand at the drawing board and his dogged determination to get things right.

No list of acknowledgments would ever be complete without some recognition for the many folks who allowed me to poke around their kitchens, shops, and dens; who tolerated my bulky photographic equipment in their living rooms; and who freely gave of their thoughts and opinions during the research phase of this book.

Introduction

ONE OF THE MOST WRENCHING PROBLEMS in the creation of this reference book was organizing it. At first I had envisioned the ideal: a simple alphabetical listing of each knife by its correct name, followed by any and all material relevant to that knife's design, construction, and use.

But once I had started collecting and filing information according to this plan, I began to perceive some inherent problems. The one that dogged me most persistently was vocabulary. Not many people know what a drawknife—or a caping knife, or a slicer—is used for. Probably they never even heard the names, so how could they associate "drawknife" with woodworking, or "caping knife" with big-game hunting, or "slicer" with a juicy boned roast? It's a little like the classic argument about the dictionary: how can you find the right word if you don't know what it is to begin with?

Duplication of material was another concern of mine. There are many generalizations that may be made about most knives, facts like the type of steel and handle material they're made from and the way they're put together. It seemed a waste of time, ink, and paper to repeat these facts in listing after listing; yet some knowledge of steels, handle materials, and construction is central to choosing any knife intelligently.

It soon became apparent that true encyclopedic organization—that is, alphabetization of subject matter—wouldn't be nearly so practical or instructive as a book written along class lines. My solution was to divide this work into five sections.

In the first section, "The Cutting Edge," you will find information on such facts as the effect of chemical hardening processes on steel and the principles and applications of the scalloped and serrated edge. Steel types, from straight carbons to the stainless series, are discussed, along with the benefits and drawbacks of each type. The jobs that stiff-bladed knives and limber-bladed knives do best are plainly outlined, as well as why wide blades make the best slicers and why slim, tapered points are undesirable on most knives. In short, this section deals in important generalizations—things that may be said about all knives—and provides a solid background for the sections that follow.

"Outdoor Knives," "Food Knives," and "Shop and Garden Knives," which represent the three common classes of edges, make up the next three sections. If knives for sport or hobby are your interest, you'll find the knife best suited to your pastime in "Outdoor Knives," along with detailed explanations of blade shapes and sizes suitable for hunting, fishing, camping, and collecting.

If you're thinking about buying a set of kitchen cutlery, or if you want to know what kind of knife to use for dicing celery or slicing a steak, look under "Food Knives." Every kind of knife you'll need to prepare, cook, and eat food is listed there.

The section on "Shop and Garden Knives" details those cutting edges that are designed for heavy work. Axes, machetes, chisels, draw-knives, and the vast array of utility pocketknives are just a few of the tools dealt with in this section.

Within each class, I have further divided the types of knives into subclasses; otherwise, I discovered, I would still have a problem with alphabetical listing. By the alphabet, a French chef's knife would follow a filet knife, and a skinning knife would follow a skin-diving knife, whereas they are miles apart in genre. So when you want to learn about a specific kind of knife, either consult the index or look through the general class of knives you're interested in. A hunting knife for deer would be in the "Outdoor Knives" section, a knife for mincing garlic would be in the "Food Knives" section, and so forth.

Remember, though, you'll be missing some important information if you don't read Part I first. And, after you have chosen your knife, the last section, "Knife Care," is a must. It contains complete instructions on how to hone a keen edge on every type of cutting tool. Also included in Part V is a thorough discussion of sharpening stones, steels, and leathers and of proper knife storage. One of the few things all knives have in common is that they must be kept sharp to perform their best, and, in a way, this final chapter on knife care sums up the theme of this book.

Once you have intelligently chosen any knife, you can count on its performance for the rest of your life—so long as you take care of it. I have a wonderful butcher knife that was my grandfather's, and a big-game hunting knife that has witnessed the passing of several thousand rugged miles (and five pairs of boots). My wife has a French chef's knife that goes with us everywhere, even on suitcase trips when she thinks she might be cooking. These knives have become old and dependable friends, and it is that kind of relationship, that kind of knowledge, that kind of craftsmanlike familiarity with a well-wrought tool, that *An Encyclopedia of Knives* aims to impart.

Part I

The Cutting Edge

THE CUTTING EDGE holds a more-than-prominent place in history—not just the kind of history that records war, politics, religion, or the development of a particular nation, but history with a capital H: the history of mankind.

It is generally accepted that our progenitors' discovery of the use and application of fire marked the flickering dawn of civilization, the dividing line between human beings as feral hominids at the mercy of the elements and thinking beings able to cope with them. The ultimate significance of fire as a tool cannot be denied, and with it arose the need for a cutting edge.

Man needed spears and arrowheads to kill game, knives to section its flesh, scrapers to cure hides, and a variety of other edges to fashion new tools of wood and bone. The importance of the cutting edge to primitive man is attested today by archaeological finds. Knives **were** commonly buried with the dead as valuable gift offerings, and the sheer numbers of edged instruments unearthed at digs indicate the high position they held as implements of early social living.

The wheel was another discovery that inaugurated a profound change in human efficiency and in our perception of mechanical principles; yet it was no more important—and perhaps less so—than the cutting edge. The wheel overcame friction and greatly increased power; but, once we emerged from the Stone Age, the edge of a plowshare tilled the land, the edge of a sword made it safe to live on, and the edge of a knife fashioned the wheel.

When we stepped from the cradle of civilization, the cutting edge established a spectacular record of contests, conquests, deaths, and defeats, from Caesar's army to the Green Berets. In many ways political history was carved with a blade, and it may be because of this bloody and popularized past that the word "knife" immediately conjures up associative words like "weapon," "fight," and "kill." Indeed, swords, stilettos, dirks, and daggers were the instruments of war, both offensive and defensive, but to assume that this was their only function obscures the larger picture. For every saber forged in a smith's furnace, there were ten axes, twenty scythes, and seventy other cutting tools that made day-to-day existence easier, more pleasant, more "civilized."

Today, the progress of investigation and invention has produced an array of tools more sophisticated, specialized, and efficient than ever before. Literally thousands of point types, steel alloys, blade shapes, handle designs, and edges grace today's cutlery, and for the most part each knife has a purpose—some job that it does better than any other knife. Yet it is the rule, not the exception, that the wrong tool is chosen for the work at hand. Meat slicers are pressed into duty as bread knives; bowie knives go camping; camping knives try to filet fish.

The problem is that the consumer—the craftsperson—is unfamiliar with the tools that are available in the trade. No one could call himself a carpenter without being able to recognize a saw, yet cooks, do-it-yourselfers, and sportsmen seldom understand those all-important tools of their trade, knives. So perhaps it's best to start this education at the very beginning, with the making of a knife.

MODERN CUTLERY MANUFACTURE

A knife may be custom made, mass produced, or machine made. Some sort of machinery is involved in the creation of any cutting tool, but the most handwork goes into the custom-made knife.

The true custom knife is one of a kind, designed by a master cutler to meet the buyer's specifications and/or special needs. The blade may be forged into shape from a blank by heating and hammering the red-hot steel on an anvil; more commonly, however, it is ground down from a blank. What distinguishes custom knife manufacture from other types is that no dies or jigs are used to shape the blade or handle. It is all handwork.

The custom knife is, understandably, the most expensive kind of cutlery, with prices for a small knife beginning at around $50. Buyers of custom knives are usually either collectors or sportsmen, especially big-game hunters.

While the mass-produced knife makes use of jigs and dies in the manufacture of handles and blades, a great deal of hand manufacture goes into this knife too. As the name implies, it is put together on an assembly line. The blade begins as a blank of quality steel, chosen by the manufacturer for the special properties of the metal. In the more common knives, those qualities are usually hardness, suppleness, and sometimes resistance to chemicals. The blank is then cut into rough shape, or punched out by a drop hammer, much the way a conductor

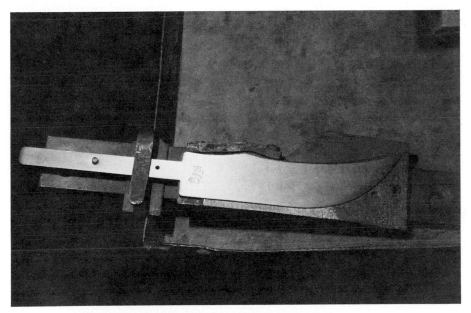

The first step in knife manufacture is roughing out the
blade from a stock of specially chosen steel.

punches a hole in a railroad ticket. Hardening and tempering of the blade take place next, processes whereby desirable properties of the knife steel are drawn out and, to some extent, improved upon.

Grinding the blade involves a series of steps, beginning with extremely coarse abrasives to reduce the knife blade to proper thickness and bevel. Successive grinding, then polishing, require finer and finer abrasives until the final finish is achieved. At this point, other parts of the knife go on: handles, hilts, pommels, and so forth. They too are ground and polished to a perfect fit, and all that is left is the sharpening.

Sharpening is usually a hand operation, and most cutlers hone a ground edge on their knives. A few manufacturers are beginning to put polished edges on their finished products. This makes for a much sharper edge, but, as you'll see, the edge on a new knife says nothing about the knife's ability to hold that edge.

A mass-produced knife retails anywhere from $2 to $40, depending on its size, the kinds of materials used, and the amount of handwork involved in putting the component parts together. Kitchen cutlery is usually the least expensive type of mass-produced knife, shop and garden tools are midrange, and sporting and collector's knives are the most expensive.

Machine-made knives involve the least handwork and consequently cost less than other knives. While it is true that the quality of materials that go into the knife—steels, handle rivets, and so forth—determines the major share of a knife's performance, the machine-made knife market is highly competitive, and many manufacturers tend to skimp on the quality of materials. For example, stainless steel knives in the $1 to $2 category simply won't take a shaving edge. They're stainless all right, but the manufacturer may not have alloyed other elements with steel to prevent a fine edge from becoming brittle and crumbling. The same may be said of sporting knives and pocketknives: "bargain" items are usually blades of mild carbon steel that take an edge easily but don't hold it. Such blades are also prone to rust, and they bend easily.

There is also an inherent problem with machine-made knives: there's little chance for quality control. When hand manufacture is at least part of the operation, there is an opportunity for a series of checks as the knife takes shape. If a bevel is improperly ground, or if rivet holes in a handle don't line up right, the blade can be remachined or discarded. When a knife pops out of a machine complete, flaws like these are often undetectable.

Aside from price, you can usually tell machine-made knives from mass-produced knives by the uniformity of the machined variety. The more handwork involved, the less standardization will be evident among knives of the same type.

CUTLERY CLASSIFICATIONS

Knife manufacturers often market their products under two or more brand names, or they may offer several lines of knives. These separate brands usually represent a "retail" or "domestic" line of cutlery, on the one hand, and "professional" knives, on the other.

Domestic cutlery is invariably made of stainless steel with synthetic handles. As the name implies, these knives are intended for general household use. They're sold in hardware and sporting-goods stores across the country and are available through mail-order houses and, occasionally, door-to-door salesmen.

Professional knives are sold to butchers, bakers, chefs, and craftspeople through wholesale outlets. The great majority of these tools have carbon steel blades and hardwood handles, though recently several manufacturers have introduced special stainless blades and synthetic handles into their professional line.

The essential difference between the two lines comes about be-

The top two knives are typical of domestic cutlery, with sculptured lines and highly polished blades. The professional knives at the bottom may not be so eye-appealing, but they make for superior cutting tools. (Case, Queen, Case, Queen)

cause retail sales depend heavily on looks and endurance. Consequently, retail lines of knives are designed with consumer eye appeal in mind, and the blade steel is chosen for its ability to maintain a shiny appearance and hold a marginal cutting edge for a long time.

Professional knives are designed for performance rather than looks, and their steel is selected for its ability to take and hold a fine cutting edge for a reasonable length of time. Professional knives don't look so ornamental as domestic knives, and they require more regular sharpening, but, provided you know how to sharpen a knife properly, they are superior tools for most cutting jobs.

THE FEATURES OF A ONE-PIECE KNIFE

Understanding knives and how to use them depends to a large extent on understanding individual knife parts and their purposes. The principal features of any knife are the blade and the handle, but those two simple parts may be given some intricate refinements.

• The butt is the rearmost part of a knife. Most kitchen cutlery has a "soft butt," a butt of rounded handle material. Some shop and garden knives and most sporting knives have a "butt cap" or "pommel," a separate butt of hard metal that protects the handle material from hard blows.

• Spacers are thin inserts of leather, plastic, or ivory inserted between the pommel and handle and the handle and hilt. They are an optional feature and are largely decorative.

• The handle lies between the butt and the hilt. Handles may be bone, metal, synthetic, wood, leather, or some combination of these. They may be made of one or two pieces, depending on the type of tang the knife has.

• The tang is the unsharpened rearward extension of the blade to which the handle is affixed.

• The guard, hilt, or bolster is the dividing line between blade and handle. Guards or hilts extend out beyond the handle. A long extension or "ear" on the guard is called a quillon. When a knife has no guard, it sometimes has a bolster for strength. The bolster is best thought of as a guard with the ears ground away.

• The choil is a cutout in the blade or handle, designed to accommodate a finger or fingers for more delicate control of the blade.

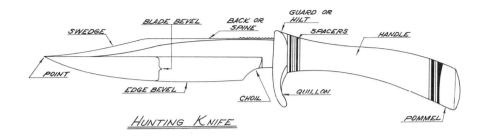

HUNTING KNIFE

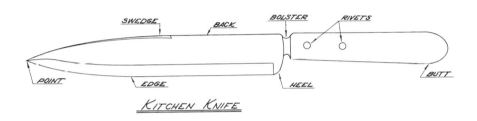

KITCHEN KNIFE

• The heel is formed by an edge that lies below the bottom line of a handle.

• The blade is one piece of steel, but it too has its subdivisions. The back or spine of a blade is the unsharpened edge or top of the blade. When a blade is sharpened on both edges, the spine is then defined as the thickest part of the blade.

• If the spine has a blade bevel from the point of the knife rearward, this is called a swedge, swage, or false edge.

• The primary bevel or blade bevel is that portion of the original steel stock that has been ground down to taper to the cutting edge.

• The edge bevel is the true cutting edge; it is the microscopic portion of the leading edge that has been ground and polished until it forms a sharp, clean V.

• The point of a knife lies at the tip of the blade. It may take any number of shapes, depending on the function of the tool.

FOLDERS AND JACKKNIVES

Like one-piece knives, folders consist basically of blade and handle, but constructing a hinged blade that is strong and locks in place is complex, requiring many more features.

• Butts or pommels are used only when the blade or blades open in one direction. When blades oppose each other, bolsters lie at both ends. The bolster on a folding knife is quite different from the bolster on a one-piece knife. Bolsters on folders are two strong fingernail-shaped side plates that are locked tight by the end rivet. They firm up the blade and prevent it from wobbling, and they are a primary anchoring point for the whole knife assembly.

• The handle on a folder does triple duty as sheath, handle, and spring mechanism. Consequently, it's quite complex. The side plate is the exterior trim of the handle. It is commonly bone, mother-of-pearl, wood, or synthetic. The side plate and bolsters are fastened to the bolster lining, which is a thin brass plate.

• The spring is a flat tongue of spring steel kept under pressure by the rivet assembly. One spring can handle two opposing blades. On a four-bladed knife, two springs are needed, and another brass plate called a center scale separates them. The rest of the knife is exactly what has been described up to now: bolster lining, side plate, and bolsters, held in place by rivets.

EXPLODED DIAGRAM OF A POCKET KNIFE

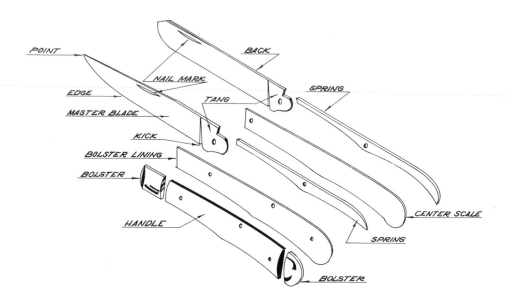

• The end rivet is the most important part of a folder, since it is both the hinge on which the blade swings and an anchoring point for the bolster and the entire handle assembly.

• The blade of a pocketknife has the same nomenclature as a one-piece knife. It has a back, point, swedge, blade bevel, edge bevel, and tang. In addition, it has a nail mark to fit a fingernail for extraction and a "kick." The kick is a downward extension of the tang whose purpose is to prevent the knife from folding so far into the handle that the nail mark can't be reached. As is true for one-piece knives, there is a wide variety of blade shapes and points for folding knives.

THE FUNCTION OF KNIFE PARTS

To find the knife that incorporated *all* the parts previously outlined would be to find a real collector's item. These features are more like options; they may or may not be incorporated into a knife's design. They are more than just frills, though, for the presence or absence of many of these parts defines the knife's function.

Butts

A butt in lieu of a cap or pommel is common on food knives. These knives should never be used for prying or wedging, particularly not by being struck on the butt, since the handle is not strong enough to withstand the shock. Absorbing such a shock is the job of a pommel.

Pommels are recommended for sporting knives and any shop knives in which the handle is breakable and the knives must be frequently struck on the butt. While pommels do sometimes ornament table carvers, on kitchenware they serve only as a catchall for foodstuffs and germs.

Because pommels are designed to bear the brunt of a blow, they should be made of hard metal. Alloys of such metals as aluminum, brass, steel, stainless steel, and silver are some of the better pommel materials.

Any knife that has a pommel must also have a tang that extends through the handle to meet it, since the whole point of a pommel is to direct the shock of a strike to the blade without impact to the handle material.

The pommel may be affixed to the tang by pinning, brazing, or forcing the cap over the tang, or by using a keyed nut that is screwed onto the threaded tang. There should be no play in the pommel, and all pommel fittings and joints should be so smooth and uniform as to appear one piece.

Spacers

Spacers are generally found only on knives that are intended, in part at least, as art or ornaments. Their original function was to hold the handle firmly in place. A tough though pliable material like leather was placed over the tang and between the pommel and handle and the handle and guard. When the pommel was pressed in place and affixed, the resistance to the compression of the spacers held the handle tight by friction. Modern knife design has eliminated the need for spacers, though they do dress up the looks of a carving set or custom hunting knife.

Handles

Handle material on knives can get quite fanciful, so it's best to begin by separating art from craft. In the realm of decorative and collector's knives, handles have been crafted from ivory, jade, wolf jaws, deer hoofs, and, by way of a real conversation piece, oozuk, the penis bone of the walrus.

In terms of working commercial cutlery, however, it's possible to narrow handle material down to more practical alternatives.

• Steel, ground and machined into a handle from the same blank that forms the blade, makes for the toughest handle. It will never

Metal handles are popular on tableware and ornamental cutlery. The handle is virtually indestructible, but it is extremely conductive of cold, heat, and electricity, and it is quite slippery unless checkered or knurled. (Federal, NA)

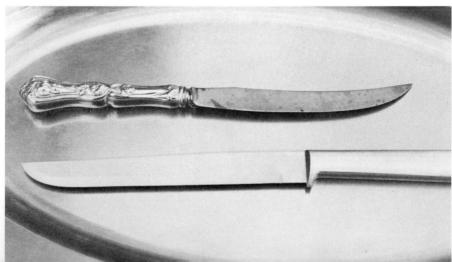

split, warp, or crack. But the conductive properties of metal make it a poor choice for knives used around a hot kitchen, in the cold outdoors, or around electrical wires. A steel handle is a wise choice for throwing knives because of its strength; for skin diver's knives because water won't split or crack it; and for flatware, for the sake of appearance and the punishment endured in dishwashers.

• Wood is a common handle material on kitchen cutlery. Hardwoods are preferable to softwoods like pine or fir because they're more heat resistant and they absorb less water. Consequently, they're less prone to burn, crack, or warp.

Common woods used in knife handles are maple, rosewood, birch, and walnut. The best wood handles are made of Brazilian or African rosewood. When evaluating a wooden handle, remember that your fingernail will dent softwoods. It won't scratch a hardwood.

The most durable wood handles are two piece, affixed to a full tang by rivets. One-piece wood handles have a habit of splitting, then falling apart.

The advantages of a wood handle are that, first, it won't conduct heat or cold and, second, it is relatively slip resistant. It rests comfortably in a wet or greasy hand and stays there while you slice the potatoes.

One disadvantage of wood is that it isn't particularly shock resistant. Wood handles on chopping tools like cleavers and woodcutters like chisels often split under normal use. Wood handles will also split, crack, or warp after too many hours in the dishwasher or too long

Wooden handles are as popular today as ever, owing to their pleasing appearance and comfortable feel. They aren't faultless, though; wood pores hold the potential for bacterial growth, and this material won't withstand impact or long immersion in water. (E. A. Berg, Gustav Ern, Normark, Buck)

a soaking in the sink. In fact, most manufacturers of wood-handled knives suggest that you wash and dry them separately to shorten the time they spend in the water. Too, because all woods are porous, wooden handles can harbor germs, and the departments of health in several states have banned their use in food-preparation businesses.

• The term "synthetic" encompasses a wide range of handle materials, from hard shell plastic to vinyl and Pakkawood. When these materials were synthesized in laboratories, inventors patented names along with chemical processes. There is, therefore, a proliferation of odd-sounding labels that say little about the qualities of the material you're dealing with.

Some synthetics make excellent knife handles; others crack or burn easily and aren't worth investing in.

Shell plastic handles are exactly what the name implies: a hard, hollow handle, riveted or glued to the tang. They burn and break easily.

The most practical synthetic handles are usually some derivative of plastic. They'll hold up in a dishwasher, and they can take impact. Without checkering, however, they're slippery, and they're moderately conductive of heat and cold. (Hull, Buck, Cutco, Centurion)

Solid plastic or vinyl handles are stronger and better, though you should be careful of brittleness. A plastic handle that can't be whittled with a sharp knife is probably too brittle to withstand any impact, and impact resistance is the quality that makes plastic desirable on chisels, cleavers, and hunting knives. It is also acceptable on fish, filet, and oyster knives, since it is unaffected by salt water. Plastic handles would be desirable around the kitchen, since they can be cleaned to a virtually germ-free state, save for one thing: they melt or burn easily. Just the rim of a hot skillet is enough to score them deeply in the blink of an eye. Plastic is also notoriously slippery, so if you choose this synthetic, you would be wise to look for a handle with a raised pattern for a better grip.

A good kitchen synthetic in modern use is a material called Pakkawood. It is made by impregnating plastic into wood. The resulting material has the pleasing appearance of wood; is dishwasher safe and burn resistant; and, because the pores are filled with plastic, is also sanitary.

Rubber or rubberlike synthetics account for the handles on most skin-diving knives, on some of the newer lines of butcher knives, and on knives used around electrical wiring. They're waterproof and, because of their sandpaperlike finish, highly slip resistant. Like vinyl, however, this material burns and scores easily.

• Bone and horn handles are mostly used on knives that function

Bone and staghorn handles are popular on sporting knives and decorative tableware. The gnarly surface provides an attractive appearance as well as a firm grip, but bone material has only slightly more impact strength than wood does, and it doesn't fare well in hot water. (Puma, NA, Case, Case)

in part as decorative objects—for example, on some carving knives and sporting knives. This material is rather brittle and can't take much impact, nor does it fare well in a dishwasher. Staghorn, with its knurled, warty surface, makes for a good, nonslip grip. All bone and horn material is moderately conductive of heat and cold.

• Leather handles are most commonly found on sporting knives. They are a laminate of washerlike doughnuts of leather stacked on a rattail or partial tang and held tight by a pommel. Leather is an excellent handle material in that it is nonconductive of heat and electricity. It is also soft, comfortable to the touch, and slip resistant, but it will not endure immersion in water, and its porous nature all but precludes effective cleaning.

• Handle shapes and designs should be assessed with the purpose of the knife in mind. A bread knife, for example, is always used to cut down, so an enlarged butt, some suggestion of a hilt or guard, and even finger cutouts along the lower part of the handle are functional. This is not the case with a paring knife. In use, a paring knife twists, turns, and rolls in your hand, and graceful curves and notches for thumb and forefinger wouldn't allow for many of the cuts.

Remember that the more precisely a handle fits your grip in one position, the more uncomfortable and awkward it will be in another. Pay particular attention to odd-shaped handles if you're left-handed. Many sculptured handles are made for the right hand only.

In general, then, a knife handle with graceful curves, smooth niches for fingers, and striking lines makes for an intriguing and valuable investment for a collector, but when it comes to a working knife it's best to keep the handle design simple, safe, and in accord with its function.

Also be sure to note the length of the handle on small knives like paring knives, clam knives, and bird-hunting knives. Perhaps out of some sense of visual balance, many of these short-bladed knives have handles that are too small to fit comfortably in your hand. You need that full, comfortable fit for cutting control.

Another aspect of fit is how well the handle mates with the rest of the knife. The handle material should meet the tang, rivets, pommel, and hilt or bolster so perfectly that it appears to be one piece. If there is any space in the joint, it will collect and hold water, which will warp or crack the handle and corrode the metal, or it may become clogged with foodstuffs and be a potential source of germs.

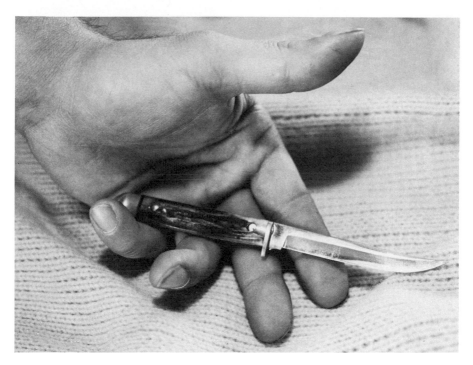

Extensively sculptured handles can often be held only one way, and handles that are too small don't afford a positive grip. Too-small handles often come attached to short-bladed knives.

Guards and Bolsters

Guards have a place on two classes of knives, those intended to be used as weapons (combat knives) and those in which the blade could conceivably be out of sight when in use.

The combat class of knives have the biggest guards, with long quillons to protect the user's hand from an opponent's edge. Sporting knives, especially hunting and skin-diving knives, are often out of sight when in use, as they are when cleaning deep inside the chest cavity of a big-game animal or when prying loose a piece of coral. In both cases, a guard prevents fingers from inadvertently slipping down on the sharpened edge. Guards on sporting knives need only be large enough to prevent this slippage. The long quillons of the combat knife would be something of a disadvantage—they would either get in the way of work or hang up in clothing or gear.

Guards are not common on food knives since they perform no function and become another repository for foodstuffs. A smooth bolster is the modern substitute. It strengthens the knife at critical blade-handle juncture, and, so long as it is well fitted, it is easily cleaned.

Tangs

There are five basic tang designs, all of which should be part of the original blade material rather than a weld or other mating of two separate parts.

• The push tang is a short rearward extension of the blade onto which the handle is forced or molded. The forced handle is held in place either by friction or by a pin. In general, push tangs are undesirable. They don't reach far enough into the handle to withstand

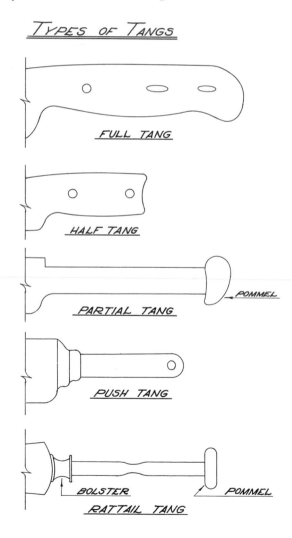

TYPES OF TANGS

FULL TANG

HALF TANG

PARTIAL TANG   *POMMEL*

PUSH TANG

BOLSTER   *POMMEL*

RATTAIL TANG

the leverage created as you cut, and they become loose and separate from the handle material when introduced to moisture.

• The rattail or round tang is stronger than the push tang, so long as it extends through the handle and is attached to a pommel. This tang is used in conjunction with one-piece handles. The handle material is center-drilled to accommodate the tang, and the pommel is held in place either by a nut threaded to the tang or by a weld.

• The full tang extends through the handle to the butt. Two handle slabs are attached to the tang by rivets. This is a strong handle design, though it is not particularly durable under impact unless a pommel graces the butt.

• The half tang extends the full depth of the handle, but reaches only halfway between hilt and butt. The handle is usually held to the tang by rivets. It is commonly found on less expensive kitchen cutlery, since it allows the manufacturer to save a few cents on steel. It is not the strongest type of construction. Blade leverage as you cut causes the

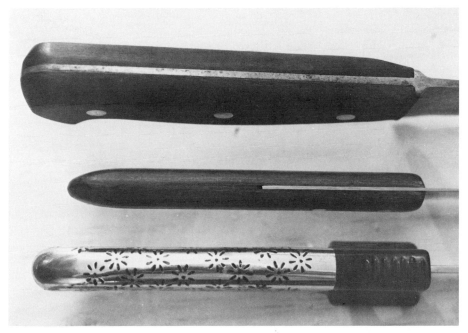

Full, half, and push tangs with the handle in place. Push tangs are common when appearance is important, since they afford the opportunity for extensive decoration.

steel to work against the handle material, when in fact the tang should be an integral part of the handle. Also, this type of handle can't withstand impact.

• The partial tang is a ground-down full tang that extends through the handle to the pommel. It is stronger than the rattail tang because there is more steel to it. Partial tangs usually grace quality knives with one-piece handles, like the best of the ornamental table carvers and certain hunting knives.

Choils

There are parallels to be drawn between sculptured handles and choils in knife blades, for the presence of both features limits the number of ways in which a knife may be comfortably held. Generally, choils have a place when there is delicate work to be done with the tip of the knife. Also, a choil on the spine is less likely to be bothersome than a choil on the cutting edge.

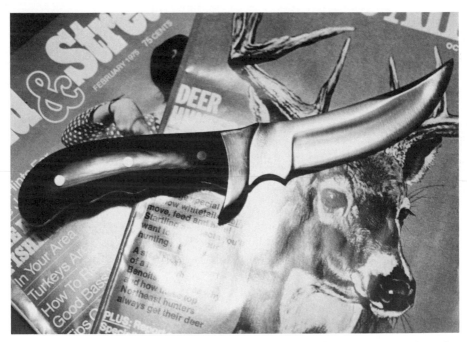

Choils are most common—and practical—on sporting knives. They allow the user more exact control of the blade, particularly near the tip. (Buck)

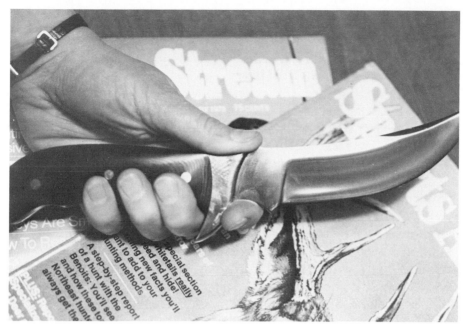

*The opposing thumb/forefinger grip on the blade made possible by a
choil permits you to make precision cuts.*

Heels

The purpose of a heel is to provide knuckle room between the
handle of a knife and a cutting board. It is a blessing on most slicing
knives, though a heel on too short a knife tends to get hung up in the
material being cut. With a short blade you overreach your stroke and
end up trying to cut with the blunt steel heel.

Balance

Although the blade does the cutting, your hand controls the blade.
Blade control is promoted by a knife that is designed to be slightly
heavy in the handle. To ascertain if this weighting exists, rest the
guard or bolster of a knife on your forefinger. The knife blade should
tip up and the handle down. This feel of balance is also called the hang.
The longer and more unwieldy a knife is, the more important its hang.
To obtain this kind of balance in a long-bladed knife requires special
efforts in engineering, since there's a lot of steel and a lot of leverage
out beyond the bolster. A large knife with proper hang means good-
quality cutlery.

Like all rules, this one has exceptions. Throwing knives and some combat knives, as well as knives designed for free chopping like cleavers and machetes, should be blade heavy.

FOLDING KNIVES

Most of the caveats applicable to one-piece knives work for folders, too. Folders, however, have more parts, so there are extra features to consider when determining how the knife will perform.

Folders are inherently weaker than one-piece knives, because the blade or blades are pinned by a hinge rather than being part of the handle and because they have a very short tang.

The strongest folders will have only one blade. Their strength is derived from the narrowness of the span between the blade bolsters and from the lack of a hinge on the butt. Folders with opposing blades rate next in strength, followed by knives with two blades that swing on one hinge, followed by those with two opposing blades, and so on. The more blades that swing on an end rivet, the weaker the knife will be. This is a law of leverage.

Strength is also indicated in a folder by a tight fit between all parts. The easiest way to assess a tight fit is with the master, or longest, blade. With the blade open, there should be no side-to-side wobble if you work the tip against a fixed surface.

Another test of quality is the ease with which the blade opens. Obviously, the blade will fit snugly if the end rivet is crimped drumhead tight against the bolsters—but that too snug fit will also tend to jam the blade, which will generally be hard to open. A folding blade that fits tightly and opens easily is made right, at least for starters.

How long the blade will remain tight depends on the excellence of the craftsmanship and on the materals used in construction. When materials like brass and nickel silver are spot-welded to form the bolster, you have top quality. When low-grade steel is crimped in place, the blade will loosen under the strain of moderate use. Obviously the buyer isn't in a position to know the materials and craftsmanship that go into a pocketknife. Many of the features are hidden from view, and you would need a laboratory analysis to identify the metals used. But there are other indications of quality.

Price is one. A good folder is going to cost more than a cheap import. In addition, top-notch folders are often packed individually, and their boxes contain data on material and construction provided by the manufacturer.

The tuning of the knife is another yardstick. When folders are fully assembled—a procedure that involves about half handwork and half machining—the final step before packaging is "tuning," whereby craftspeople evaluate and adjust the knife until "it can walk and talk."

A finely tuned folder should snap open and closed with a solid-sounding click. Open, the spring should line up perfectly with the back of the blade, and the blade should be aligned perfectly with the handle. Closed, the nail nick should be easy to grasp and the kick should keep the point of the blade inside the line of the handle so it can't snag clothing or hands. In the closed position, the spring should line up perfectly with the back of the handle.

• Hilts or guards occasionally grace one-bladed folders. The less expensive knives have guards that are part of the bolster. More expensive folders have guards that fold into, or in line with, the handle when the blade is closed. I have owned and used both types of knives, and I find any sort of hilt bothersome on a folder. The bolster hilts snag in your clothing, and the knife refuses to lie comfortably in your pocket. The folding hilts are just another piece of machinery to go haywire. The one type of folder on which a hilt *may* be justified is one used as a big-game knife, though I still feel that the need is debatable at best.

• Locks are another feature incorporated into single-bladed knives. They usually work by means of the spring mechanism; a sear on the spring jams into a hole in the blade tang, or a sear on the blade jams into the spring.

Because of its greater leverage, the longer the blade on a folder, the more need there is for a lock as a safety feature. A strong spring will hold a three-inch blade firmly and discourage accidental closing. But, as the tip gets further and further away from the end rivet, springs can't be made strong enough to put sufficient pressure on the tiny blade tang. Without a lock, a long blade can close on your fingers without warning.

Another blade that should have a lock is a screwdriver blade on a general-purpose knife. Any blade that is subject to pressure in line with the handle is likely to close on your hand, and I have had more cuts from screwdriver blades and awls than I care to recollect.

THE KNIFE BLADE

A knife is a tool of integrated parts. If it has a weak or poorly shaped handle, for example, or wears long quillons for no reason, it won't function properly. Still, if there is a "most" important part of a knife —a heart—it is the blade.

With the exception of silver tableware, which is really as ornamental as it is utilitarian, knife blades are made of steel. Steel is an alloy of iron and carbon.

Steel types differ as much and as subtly as do brands and models of cars, or the varieties of material that fall under the label "plastics." Depending on the ratio of carbon to iron, steel can be soft enough to be worked with a hammer—or so hard that only the hardest material known on earth, a diamond, is capable of scoring or cutting it.

Steel for knife blades should fall between these two extremes and should possess three properties: toughness, hardness, and corrosion resistance. Toughness is best defined as the ability to recover from bending and stress without breaking. Hardness has to do with steel's ability to hold an edge. This edge must be much harder than the materials the blade will cut, or those materials themselves will cut the fine edge and dull it. Corrosion resistance refers to the steel's ability to withstand certain chemicals without rusting, pitting, or staining.

Toughness is needed when the knife is called upon to pry, resist impact, or bone. Prying with a knife is often necessary when you are carving or butchering—when, for example, you have to separate bone joints. Impact situations occur around the shop and garden and in butchering. Axes and cleavers are examples of "impact" knives. Fileting and boning require a knife that can bend to conform to odd angles, yet return to its original shape. Steel "toughness," "springiness," or "suppleness" lends this quality.

Steel must also be hard enough to hold an edge well. A "mild" or low-carbon steel can be bent, pounded, and dented with a hammer. It is considered a soft steel. While it is extremely easy to grind and hone an edge on soft steel, the very ease with which it can be sharpened is an indication of how easily it will become unsharpened. Bone, for example, is harder than mild steel. Draw a soft-steel knife across a hambone and it is immediately dulled. Even materials that are softer than the steel—hair, wood, meat—will work against a fine edge on mild steel and dull it quickly. There's also the "rollover" problem. When you hone soft steel to shaving sharpness, the edge is too soft to be stiff and a minuscule burr will roll off the edge when you cut. The effect is the same as cutting with a dull knife.

None of these problems arise with hard, high-carbon steel, but this alloy, too, has its limits. When so much carbon is present that steel hardness approaches that of a diamond, it is virtually impossible to sharpen the blade by conventional means. There is no economical abrasive material to grind and cut the steel. The sharpening stones that are within the means of a cook or sportsman are so close to the knife's hardness that it takes literally hours of stroking and stropping to get an edge. There is yet another problem. As the percentage of carbon increases in the iron (essentially, the more carbon present, the harder the steel), toughness decreases. The ability to bend and recover from stress is replaced by crystalline brittleness; thus, the slightest impact or gentlest prying will flake chips off the cutting edge or break the blade like a matchstick. Diamonds are the hardest things on earth, but they're not the toughest. Strike one with a hammer and it will shatter like glass. The same thing is true of high-carbon steel. A "hard" knife is desirable for its edge-holding characteristics, but there are definite limits to the amount of hardness that is desirable.

There's another important consideration in choosing a knife: corrosion resistance. Rust, the most common form of corrosion, is the result of iron combining with oxygen to create a compound called ferrous oxide. The chemical reaction is encouraged and hastened by other chemicals and compounds present in the air and in the materials being cut, especially salt and water. Blood, for example, contains both salt and water.

Appearances alone will lead you to choose a knife with no traces of rust, but you should know that a rust-encased blade is not going to cut efficiently either. The rough corrosion along the blade sets up friction and drag, making a precise stroke difficult. And even though a knife made of easily corroded steel may appear to be free of rust, along the cutting edge small pits and jagged ridges, visible through a microscope, may have been eaten into the metal, which should form a straight, smooth V. This smaller-scale corrosion, too, makes precision cutting impossible.

The ideal knife, then, would be tough enough to bend without breaking, yet would neither shatter nor dent under impact. It would be hard enough to hold an edge against the materials it is designed to cut and slice, but soft enough to be sharpened by a commercial stone. And it would never corrode. Like all things in heaven and earth, this ideal is virtually unattainable.

Each of these qualities—toughness, hardness, and corrosion resistance—can be achieved individually in steel by further alloying with other materials. The addition of small amounts of silicon and manganese will make a knife that's supertough. A high carbon content will make diamond-hard steel. And the addition of chromium to steel creates "stainless" steel with a high degree of corrosion resistance. But it is nearly impossible to have a perfect balance of all three qualities at the same time.

When you toughen steel, you reduce its abrasion resistance. The knife sharpens easily, but it dulls quickly.

When you harden steel, you increase abrasion resistance, but you also increase its brittleness and this in turn reduces its toughness.

When you add chromium to steel, the element that makes it stainless, you also increase its hardness to a point where it is difficult to sharpen. In fact, the steel may become so brittle that it will not hold an edge. Tiny nicks and cracks crumble along the fine point of the V. They are invisible to the naked eye but appear plainly under a microscope.

I should, however, point out that the robbing-Peter-to-pay-Paul consequences of alloying cutlery steel are not insurmountable. It is possible to shuffle alloys and chemicals and heat treatments around to achieve near-perfection, but this kind of quality is extremely expensive.

Custom knife makers tinker with alloy content and heat tempering to produce magnificent blades, but their products are too costly for the average consumer. Space technology has spun off steels with perfect properties for knife blades, but these alloys are literally worth their weight in gold. A more common example of such supersteel lies in the safety razor blade. It's a type of stainless, it can be bent nearly in half without breaking, yet it holds the keenest of all edges. Still, a blade of several ounces of razor steel would be far too expensive for common cutlery. Granted, there are those who think the $20,000 difference between a Rolls-Royce and a Ford is worth it when it comes to basic transportation and, indeed, there is a vast difference in quality. But most of us can't afford the ratio of quality gained for money spent. When you go beyond $5,000 for a set of dependable wheels, you're buying a lot of intangibles, and the same may be said for knives. Commercial cutlery, with its minor faults, is inexpensive but eminently utilitarian —provided you know what you're buying.

• Straight-carbon blades are made of a steel mixture that is primarily carbon and iron. They contain between 50 and 80 parts of carbon per 1,000 parts of iron. The lower carbon blade would tend to be "soft." It would sharpen easily, but it would lose its edge quickly, too. It would bend without breaking, but it might not recover from an extreme bend and could develop a kink.

A blade of 80 parts carbon would be difficult to sharpen, but it would hold an edge well. It would tend to be brittle, but it would never develop a kink.

Carbon blades do not stay shiny like stainless steel blades. If you don't care for them, they will eventually rust. If you care for them, they will stain to a dull pewter color.

Given the sharpening tools most of us have, a carbon blade is easiest to sharpen and will take and hold the finest edge. Straight-carbon blades normally grace that class of knives known as "professional" cutlery—the tools used by butchers and chefs, a class of users which in itself is a comment on their quality.

• Stainless steel is primarily a mixture of iron and chromium. Stainless steel isn't really impossible to stain; many household chemicals will etch or corrode it. But it does stain less than straight carbons, and its bright, shiny appearance makes it popular.

There are many types of stainless alloys possible, but the compound most acceptable for cutlery is the so-called "400 series," which has between 11.5 percent and 29.5 percent chromium alloyed with steel and a trace of carbon. Of that series, "440-C," with 17 percent to 19 percent chromium content, is generally accepted as the finest for knife blades.

In many ways the addition of chrome brings out the best in steel. It increases hardness and abrasion resistance, and it retards the formation of crystal growth as the molten steel cools. This in turn promotes toughness in the finished blade. It is also undeniably good-looking, either polished to a mirror finish or buffed to the dull gray sheen of a satin finish. Stainless steel also has high tensile strength (which means, essentially, that, like taffy, it is highly resistant to being pulled apart) and it is, of course, corrosion resistant.

Stainless is not, however, without some faults. For one thing, unalloyed stainless is so hard that it's difficult to resharpen once it loses its edge, and inferior stainless can be brittle. Brittle stainless will not hold a fine, polished edge.

Because of its stainless nature, this steel is the best choice for blades used to cut highly corrosive materials like citrus fruits. It's also the steel for use around salt water, and its edge-holding ability makes it desirable on knives with a serrated or scalloped edge and for those that must be kept shiny for appearance's sake.

Steel Alloys

Other elements may be added to either straight carbons or stainless steels to create secondary characteristics in the metal. The following is a sampling of those elements and the effect they have on the nature of the blade:

• Vanadium is added to steel in minute quantities of between 0.12 percent and 0.20 percent. It promotes control of grain size and the steel's ability to be fire hardened. It thus retards internal stress in the blade and makes it less brittle.

• Nickel increases the tensile strength and toughness of steel, but in small quantities it will not increase hardness. It is one of the more desirable alloys of stainless steel. If, however, large amounts (24 percent and over) of nickel are added, the steel becomes so hard that it cannot be worked. This undesirable point of alloying can be detected because the steel becomes nonmagnetic.

• Molybdenum in small amounts (0.10 percent to 2 percent) increases corrosion resistance, toughness, and the capacity to be fire hardened, but it also increases general hardness so that the blade becomes difficult to sharpen. It is a valuable additive to straight carbons, but of doubtful benefit in stainless steel.

• Tungsten promotes a hard, fine-grain steel that holds a sharp cutting edge. But the edge is very difficult to rehone once it dulls. Tungsten alloys are usually best suited to tools like drill bits and steel chisels.

• Laminated steel isn't really an alloy, but it deserves mention and this seems the most logical spot. It amounts to a thin core of steel, bonded between two outer layers of soft steel. This produces a thin edge, one that is easy to sharpen and holds its keenness a long time. It is reinforced by tough outer layers that are easily removed by a sharpening stone. Like the laminates found in plywood, this lends tremendous springiness and strength to the blade.

The idea of lamination is excellent. The quality of the blade is, of course, determined by the types of steel used in the laminate and by the strength of the bonding process. But if it all hangs together, a laminated blade is tops. These blades are, however, too expensive for commercial cutlers to produce, which explains, perhaps, why you don't see them often. One can only hope that someday someone will discover how to laminate blades cheaply. The process is a wonderful answer to a lot of problems inherent in one-piece blades.

Chemical and Heat Treatments

The quality and nature of the steel that goes into a knife blade determine a great deal of that blade's characteristics. Those characteristics can be further altered and improved by several chemical and heat treatments.

It should be noted that, while these treatments increase qualities like toughness and hardness, the ability to be toughened and hardened must be inherent in the steel to begin with. All the tempering in Pittsburgh won't change an inferior steel.

• Case hardening is a cheap way to make soft steel hard while maintaining toughness. To case-harden steel, low-carbon stock is immersed in a below-critical-temperature bath of molten sodium cyanide, then quenched in water, brine, or oil. (The critical point or critical temperature is that point of heating at which some definite change takes place in the physical properties of steel. This point in cutlery steel generally falls between 1,400 and 1,600 degrees Fahrenheit, not enough to turn the steel cherry red.) The result is a very hard skin or casing over the soft steel between 0.10 and 0.015 inches thick. The metal core remains soft.

When you sharpen a case-hardened knife, you're removing the hard coating and exposing the soft steel on the cutting edge. Obviously, this is not desirable. Case hardening is a poor treatment for a knife blade and is better suited to impact tools like hammers.

• Fire hardening heats the knife blade beyond the critical point of the steel. The steel is then rapidly cooled in a bath of oil, water, or brine or in a caustic solution; this process is called quenching. The effect of fire hardening is essentially to make the steel molecules more compact, thereby making the steel harder. However, internal stresses are set up in the process, making the knife brittle. Put another way, the knife steel is hard but tense, with internal molecules under a strain like a tightly wound clock spring. Fire-hardened blades must therefore be treated further—"relaxed" if you will—by a process called tempering.

• Tempering is a process whereby the internal stress is drawn from hardened steel. This is accomplished by reheating the blade to a relatively low temperature (around 500 degrees Fahrenheit) immediately after quenching.

The effect of tempering is to relax the internal stress set up by the hardening, to relax that tight spring. To some extent, hardness gained in the fire is sacrificed to reduce brittleness and increase toughness, but the end product still is a harder, tougher steel than the original untreated blank.

The Rockwell Hardness Scale

It would be misleading to attempt to say what alloy or steel type is best. There are just too many variables to deal with, considering the number of alloy materials, the various percentages in which they are added to steel, and the different temperatures possible during the hardening and tempering process. However, be assured that every cutlery manufacturer is positive that his steel is best. Manufacturers spend so much time perfecting their mixtures and treatments that exact percentages and steps are often a closely guarded company secret.

The logical question that follows is, How does a buyer ascertain the qualities of the steel in the blade he's buying? To some extent, you can't—at least, not for *all* the qualities. But you can learn something about that blade's hardness and ability to take an edge by the Rockwell Hardness Scale.

The scale is based on a standard test of steel hardness. A diamond point is forced into a finished blade under precisely regulated pressure, and the depth of the indentation is measured by sophisticated instruments. The depth of penetration is then converted to a scale, and a figure is given. A Rockwell (or RC) hardness above RC 60 will be difficult to sharpen with conventional stones. An RC below 56 won't hold an edge well.

While manufacturers may be chary of their steel blends, there's no reason for them to be secretive about the hardness of their blades, and this information should be available somewhere in their promotional literature. Remember, however, that an RC number tells you *only* about hardness. There is no regular test for edge-holding ability, brittleness, and toughness save long, hard use.

The Scratch Test

Another hardness test you can make yourself is the scratch test. It's based on the fact that a hard steel will scratch a softer steel, but the process won't work in the inverse. You surely have some knife you favor for the ease with which it takes an edge and the length of time it holds it. Remember that a blade of the same type of steel won't be scratched by your favorite, nor will the second blade scratch the first. You can also use the scratch test another way. If you have a knife that won't take an edge, try a softer blade, one that can be scratched by the hard-to-sharpen knife. If you have a knife that won't hold an edge because it's too soft, buy another that's hard cnough to scratch the soft blade.

The Blade Bevel

The blade bevel is the ground-away portion of the knife blade that tapers from the spine to the edge. The blade bevel is not the same as the cutting edge. A second bevel, called the edge bevel, is honed to the bottom of the blade bevel to make the cutting edge.

The angle of the blade bevel determines some of the characteristics of the blade. If that angle is extremely acute, the knife will have a soft spine and bend easily. As a blade bevel becomes less acute, or wider, the spine of the blade becomes stiffer, and the knife becomes stronger and more of a heavy duty tool. The blade bevel also defines the degree of sharpness that can be honed onto the edge.

The angle of the edge bevel—the fine edge put on the blade bevel— is the angle of the blade bevel. If you are working with a wide-V blade bevel, the edge bevel will constitute an even wider V. It is the narrow, slim-V edge bevel that makes for the sharper knife. Put another way, a heavy, thick-spined hunting knife can't be honed as sharp as a slim, fine-tapered carving knife.

The best knife bevels—or tapers, as they're occasionally called— have two dimensions. Viewed from straight on, eyeball-to-knife-point, they taper from spine to edge. From the top, the width of the spine diminishes toward the point.

This double taper promotes hang, since the knife will have less steel toward the blade tip. It also contributes to a perfect parabolic

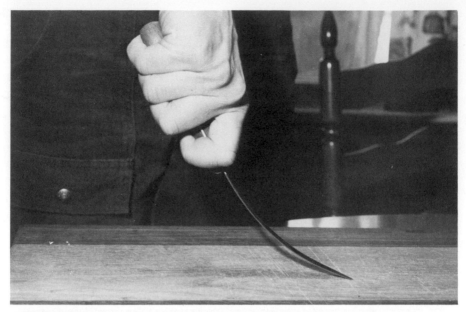

A blade that is the same thickness from tip to hilt takes a normal curve when subjected to pressure, making straight cuts, as in boning or fileting, very difficult.

Taper promotes hang as well as a parabolic bend that curves gracefully from tip to hilt in medium-limber to limber-spined blades. (Dexter, Normark)

arc in a thin-spined knife when the blade is flexed against a cutting board. The added fine control made possible by this arc makes it an extremely important feature for many food knives. The double taper also makes it easier to hone a uniform edge bevel on any knife from bolster to tip.

There are six blade bevels in general use.

• The straight bevel is a nonbevel. An edge is honed directly onto a flat blade blank. The straight bevel is most often found on food slicers and certain shop knives.

• The V grind is a uniform taper that begins at the spine of the

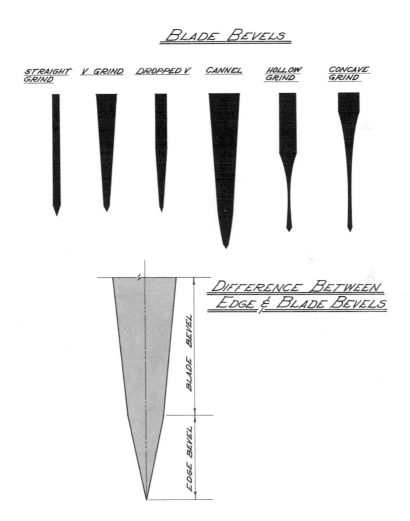

BLADE BEVELS

STRAIGHT GRIND   V GRIND   DROPPED V   CANNEL   HOLLOW GRIND   CONCAVE GRIND

DIFFERENCE BETWEEN EDGE & BLADE BEVELS

BLADE BEVEL

EDGE BEVEL

knife and drops to the edge. It is common on foreign-made kitchen cutlery, folding knife blades, and some sporting knives. This grind produces a relatively strong edge that resists chipping when it is used to chop or pry.

• The dropped V grind is a combination of a straight bevel and V grind. The straight bevel extends from the back of the knife to a point near the middle of the blade. Then a V is ground to meet the edge. This type of grind results in a very strong back and sturdy blade. It is a common blade bevel on sporting knives.

• The cannel or rolled bevel begins as a V bevel, then curves or rolls to meet the edge. A cannel can't be honed shaving sharp, but it holds its edge forever, and the blade is extremely resistant to chipping when used to chop or pry. It is usually found on heavy-duty sporting knives and shop tools.

• The hollow-ground bevel has a hollow or dish-shaped concave ground into the leading edge of the blade, below the spine. The purpose of the hollow grind is to create a substantial area of thin steel near the edge; this, in turn, facilitates sharpening. The hollow grind

Three of the most popular blade bevels: dropped V, concave, and V grinds. (Interpur, Buck, Puma)

and the concave grind are good edge bevels for knives that must be kept shaving sharp.

• The concave grind is a little like the hollow grind, except that the thickness of the steel does not dish out as it approaches the cutting edge; rather, it meets that edge in an extremely acute V. The concave grind is the easiest grind to keep sharp, but, like its close relative, the hollow grind, it makes for a weak edge that will chip deep into the blade and ruin the knife if you use it for anything but light cutting.

The Edge Bevel

The fine edge that is ground and polished on a blade bevel is called the edge bevel. The type of edge bevel and its degree of acuteness are determined by the blade bevel and by the work to which the knife will be put. Like the blade bevel, the edge bevel has two dimensions. One is its degree of acuity; the other is its conformation, or the shape the bevel takes in relation to the blade.

Acuity is best explained by imagining that you're looking at a cross-section of the blade with the aid of a microscope. In order for

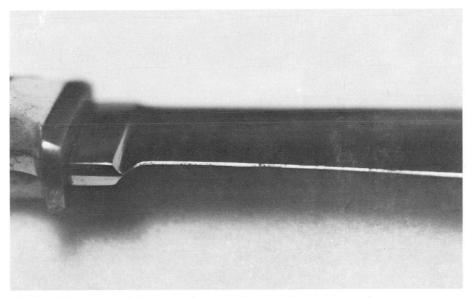

Light reflections and close-up photography reveal the true cutting power of a knife, the edge bevel. The edge bevel is a thin line of honed steel that must take a less acute angle than the blade bevel.

the edge to cut, it must come to some sort of V. As the acuity or width of the V edge varies, so does the knife's performance as a cutting tool.

The degree of bevel on an edge can range anywhere from 12 to 50 degrees. A 12-degree bevel is strictly a slicing edge, a 36-degree bevel approaches a chopping edge, and a 50-degree bevel rates as a wedging edge.

The extremely acute edge bevel is typified by a scalpel. It is unsurpassed as a slicing tool. But the fine edge on a scalpel will not endure pressure. Try to force the scalpel down or, more foolishly, chop with it, and the blade will become nicked.

Most edge bevels are between 25 and 35 degrees. At this range there is enough strength in the steel to keep the edge smooth, and the angle is acute enough to cut with relative ease. This is the edge that belongs on utility and general-purpose cutting knives of all kinds— carvers, jackknives, sporting knives, dicing knives, paring knives, and boning knives.

A chopping edge is usually between 35 and 45 degrees. It will slice soft materials, but it does this job poorly. The angle of the V is just not acute enough. But that fat V bevel has plenty of steel in back of its relatively dull leading edge, so the edge will not crumble under impact. This is the edge that belongs on axes, cleavers, and machetes.

The 50-degree bevel is a wedging bevel. Examples of tools that wedge are the maul ax, which is used to split wood, and clam knives. It's nearly impossible to slice anything with this type of bevel; it's designed to wrench things apart when the ax is backed up by plenty of pressure.

The acuity of the bevel indicates how well a knife will slice or chop. The conformation of the bevel indicates what that edge will slice or chop.

• The double-edge bevel comes to a perfect V on the cutting edge. This edge bevel is the standard, the workhorse, and 70 percent of the cutting tools you're likely to run across will wear it. If you could have one knife with one edge, this would be the one to choose, for it will do the greatest variety of jobs.

• The single-edge bevel has an off-kilter V, with one leg perpendicular to the ground. To create a single-edge bevel, only one side of the knife is honed. It is a practical edge only when used in conjunction with a straight blade bevel, but it is an excellent edge for slicing since it characteristically cuts in a straight line, while V bevels on the edge and

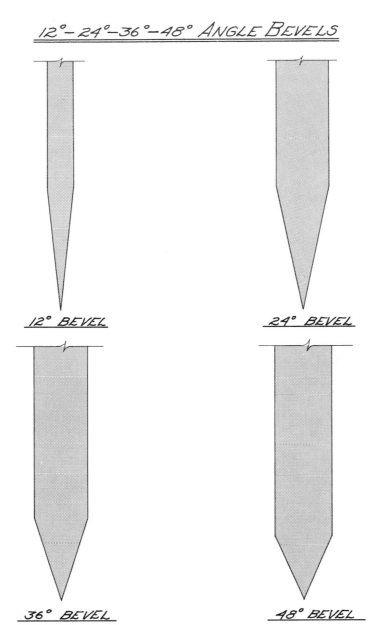

12°–24°–36°–48° ANGLE BEVELS

12° BEVEL

24° BEVEL

36° BEVEL

48° BEVEL

These drawings show edge bevels viewed cross-sectionally under a microscope. Because of its acuity, the 12-degree bevel makes for the most efficient cutting edge, but it is also the weakest and the most likely to nick or dull quickly because there is so little steel to reinforce the leading edge. As edge bevels become less acute, they are more resistant to chipping and dulling but less efficient at cutting.

blade tend to wander. The single bevel also resists being dulled by hot meats.

Surprisingly enough, the single-edge bevel is not commonly available on kitchenware, though it is perfect for slicing foods like boned roasts and cold cuts. It is common on many shop tools, from chisels to planes, scrapers to carvers. Straight, clean slicing is an important feature of this bevel when used in the wood shop (as it is in the kitchen); important, too, is its tendency to push cut material out and away as the blade moves along.

One characteristic of this edge worthy of note is that it can be used only in one direction: with the bevel facing away from the bulk of material being cut and into the scraps being shaved away. For a smooth, uniform cut, the flat of the blade must rest against the roast of beef, the block of cheese, or the block of wood. This is not so limiting or complex as it sounds, but it's a rule you must obey for a straight cut.

• Scalloped edges are a series of linked half-moons ground and sharpened along the cutting edge. The design of the scallops varies with each manufacturer, but the principle of scalloped edges remains the same: the pointed teeth act a little like a saw. As they rip through the food, more cutting is done in the hollows, which remain sharp longer than the rest of the blade, being protected from the most difficult part of the cutting by the teeth.

Scalloped edges have been promoted as never needing sharpening, but that's hogwash. All knives require regular touch-ups, those with scalloped edges included. If you buy one of these knives, make sure one side of the scallops has a perfectly flat bevel, or you'll be able to sharpen only the teeth and not the hollows.

Scalloped edges are useful for acidic foods such as tomatoes and citrus fruits, which would otherwise dull a fine straight edge. They are also handy for cutting frozen foods, bread, and cold cuts. But they simply are not suited to every cutting job in the kitchen, certain manufacturers' claims notwithstanding.

• Serrated edges are sawteeth cut into the edge of a knife. The knife cuts only in the direction the teeth point, so the most practical serrated edge will incorporate blocks of teeth that point in both directions so that the knife will cut forward and back.

Like the scalloped edge, the serrated edge is used almost exclusively for cutting food. (It is also useful for cutting rope.) In fact, this

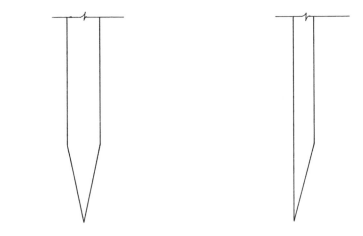

"V" OR DOUBLE-EDGE BEVEL   SINGLE-EDGE BEVEL

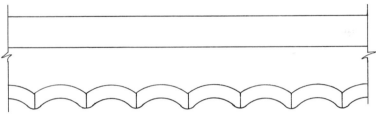

SCALLOPED EDGE

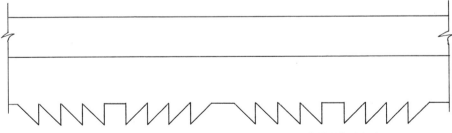

SERRATED-EDGE PATTERN

BLOCKS OF TEETH POINT IN OPPOSITE
DIRECTIONS SO KNIFE CUTS BOTH
FORWARD & BACKWARD.

Although patterns differ, the principles remain the same. The scalloped edge resembles a series of linked half-moons, and the serrated edge resembles sawteeth.

edge doesn't cut in the true sense of the word; it tears. Consequently, it has a supplementary place next to traditionally dull table flatware for use on sinewy meats like steak and roast beef, and it is excellent as a bread knife.

THE KNIFE POINT

The conformation of the tip of a knife is as integral a part of its function as the edge, handle, or bevel. Like all the other parts of a knife, the point contributes to defining the tool's function and efficiency.

A point provides entry, either in the form of a thrust or of a tiny cut. An example of thrust entry would be piercing the soft cartilage of the pelvic bone of an animal about to be butchered. Cut entry can be illustrated by the action of a surgeon's scalpel or the stroke of a gardener's grafting knife.

It's a useful rule of thumb that a knife designed for thrust entry has a long, slender point. Hence, knives fashioned as weapons characteristically have long, wicked-looking tips. The needlelike stiletto is the classic of the kind.

A slightly broader point and blade than the stiletto, equipped with a fine edge, affords easy entry and the ability to slice and cut. This type of point graces boning knives that are used to cut meat from the tight

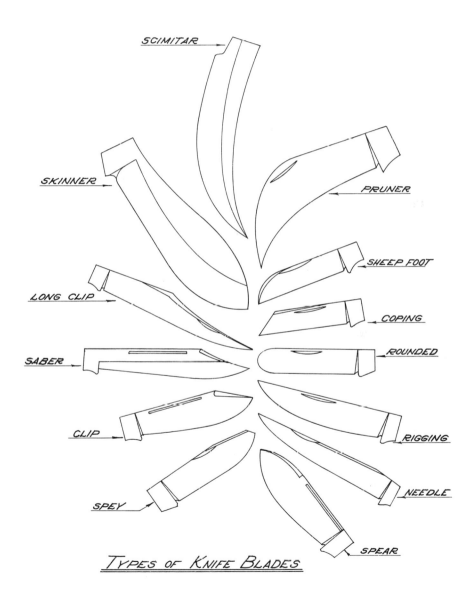

TYPES OF KNIFE BLADES

contours of bone and cartilage with a minimum of exterior slicing. Filet knives also serve the same function, and the tips of both knives are quite similar in appearance.

Contour cutting and slicing around bone are also the work of a carving knife, and the more slicing a knife is meant to do, the broader the design of its point and blade.

After the carver, in the middle range of tip shapes, come the paring and vegetable knives, with wider blades and stronger tips that can slice, penetrate, or pry, lancing out the eye of a potato or the bruised section of turnip.

Contemporary combat and survival knives have broader tips than vegetable knives. Though part of their function is self-defense, they must also serve as general-purpose survival tools. The thinness of a fine stiletto point would weaken a tip with an edge; hence the compromise.

Hunting and outdoor knives are next on the scale. Occasionally they are used to penetrate into the cavity of a fish or downed game,

Slender, upswept points belong on knives that must cut at the tip.
A blunted tip, or no tip at all, belongs on a blade that is
primarily a slicing instrument.

and their broader tips ensure that they can also be used for many jobs that require tip slicing or blade strength. An even broader tip, with its inherent strength, is the trademark of the throwing knife. Thonking home into wood at high speeds puts quite a strain on steel.

Knives used for cut entry have an extremely broad tip, with a severe pitch up or down to meet the point. They are seldom thrust. Skinning knives, castrating knives, and some butcher knives are examples in this class.

A tip that pitches down to meet a straight edge is used only for cut entry. Certain kinds of scalpels and taxidermy tools, grafting knives, and linoleum knives have this type of tip.

No point or a blunt point belongs on those kinds of knives that utilize edge alone: bread, pastry and cheese knives, clam shuckers and cleavers.

The location of a point in relation to the rest of a knife's conformation helps designate its function, too. A point in line with the blade's handle (for all practical purposes, a point that touches an imaginary center line) is the most efficient for a thrust entry. Examples of knives in this category would be combat and fighting knives, throwing knives, the master blade on a typical pocketknife, and general-purpose outdoor knives. As the line along which the point falls gets closer to the back of the knife, the tip area of the blade begins to assume a slicing as well as a probing function. Examples of this kind of blade would be kitchen utility knives, big-game hunting knives, and meat-slicing knives.

The higher the tip, the more slicing work can be done with the tip section of the blade. This is the reason for the shapes of boning and filet knives, skinning knives, and butchering knives. In some of these knife designs, the whole blade is canted upward to make the most out of the wrist-directed tip-slicing action.

At the opposite extreme, blades with a dropped tip in line with the edge are slicers, such as whittling knives, ham slicers, and bread knives, which require the stroke of your arm rather than any wrist action for cutting.

Swedges and Double Edges

A double-edge knife with two fully sharpened edges is strictly a tool of combat, and a historical one at that. Modern combat knives have a sharpened swedge, but true double edges are rare today, even when knives are designed as weapons.

A sharpened swedge—a second sharpened edge that runs halfway down the back of the knife from the point—serves to facilitate point penetration, since it slices flesh out of the way, allowing the point to drive deeper. During combat, it allows the user to cut an opponent on an upstroke.

Sharpened swedges and double edges serve no purpose on other knives and are plainly dangerous. Unsharpened swedges, however, do ornament a lot of modern cutlery.

Although a knife maker once told me that an unsharpened swedge strengthens the blade, I can't for the life of me figure out how or why.

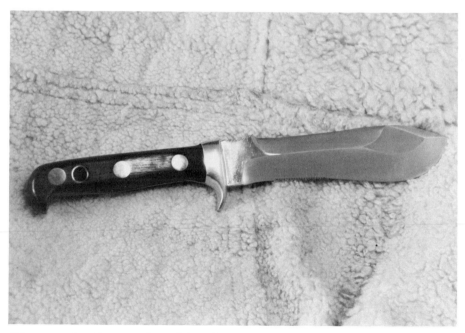

The extensive sharpened swedging defines the purpose of this knife, but note also the skinning tip; the spine, which indicates a weapon; and a hole in the handle for a lanyard. The swedge and spine are for defense, the tip design is for all-purpose cutting, and the lanyard hole allows the knife to be firmly lashed to a pole for fishing, hunting, or self-defense. It's classed as a survival knife. (Puma)

I'd guess the swedge to be a carry-over from the days when personal cutlery did double duty as a weapon of defense. In this context the sharpened swedge was needed.

At any rate, the modern unsharpened swedge does add a touch of grace and class to cutlery—though by no means should you judge the performance of a knife by its presence or absence.

Blade Dimensions

The more steel there is in a blade of a given length, the stronger that blade will be. However, because of the pitch of the blade bevel down to the edge bevel on a wide-spined knife, it takes longer to sharpen and will not hone to as keen an edge as a thin-spined knife, which meets the edge bevel at a more acute angle. Nor will a thick-spined knife slice as cleanly as a slip of steel. The severe bevel defies an even cut and forces the edge this way and that. On the other hand, a thin-bladed knife is capable only of light cutting. It will not chop, pry, or penetrate under pressure without danger of breaking.

In general, the heavier the work you expect of a blade, the thicker its spine should be. Don't expect a kitchen knife to endure a camping trip—and don't expect a hunting knife to lop off perfect, thin slices of roast beef. In both cases, you have the wrong knife for the job.

Blade length, for the most part, should be determined by the amount of work that's to be done at the tip. The farther the tip is from the handle and your hand, the less control you'll have over it. For precise—and safe—tip work, select a short-bladed knife. Conversely, when a knife is strictly a slicer, you'll get the most uniform cutting action if you can complete the slice in one stroke. Hence, slicers, carvers, and butcher knives are always long, with blades up to 12 and 14 inches.

Blade depth—that is, the distance between spine and edge—and its function can best be understood by comparing an ice pick and a cleaver. Stick an ice pick into meat and it can be twirled like a pinwheel. Partially cleave a piece of meat, and you'll find it impossible to cut in anything but a straight line.

Shallow-bladed knives are comparable to ice picks. They are for contour cutting, when there are bends, bones, and curves to work around. Filet knives and boning knives are classic examples. But shallow-bladed knives resist cutting in a straight line. A blade with a lot of depth to it tracks like a cleaver as it cuts. The flat side of the blade, riding against the bulk of the material being cut, resists twisting and acts like a guide. The result is uniform slices.

Typical examples of deep-bladed slicers would be the French chef's knife for vegetables and the butcher knife for meat. The most common household slicer, the carving knife, is something of a compromise. Its depth is midway between a filet knife and a butcher knife because it's called upon for slicing and a certain amount of contour cutting as well—for example, around the breast of a turkey or the bones of a standing rib roast.

Blade Finishes

The finish on a blade is both decorative and protective. Blades look better when they're polished to a dull sheen or silver brightness, but along with improving their appearance polishing removes small scratches that would otherwise encourage corrosion. Water beads on a polished blade and is easily wiped off. Still another reason for polishing is smoothness. A polished blade slides through the material being cut; an unpolished blade drags.

• The mirror finish on a knife is the most common, and it usually graces stainless steels. Buffing wheels with increasingly finer grades of abrasives are used to create a smooth, shiny surface that reflects like a mirror.

This finish is undeniably good-looking, but subsequent sharpenings are bound to mar the surface with scratches. Unless you have access to buffing wheels, no amount of polishing will remove them either, and an otherwise good knife appears old and beat up.

• The satin finish falls a few polishing steps short of the mirror finish. It is a common finish on straight carbon blades and is becoming more common on stainless blades.

The satin finish is glass smooth, but, rather than reflecting like a mirror, it glows with a dull gray sheen. Because it is not highly reflective, sharpening scratches are virtually unnoticeable and the blade maintains its good looks over the years.

• The blued finish is common on shop and garden tools and some sporting and combat knives. It is used exclusively on carbon blades. To achieve a blued finish, the polished steel is treated with a mild acid that oxidizes the bare surface, creating a thin blue "skin" that acts as a barrier to corrosion.

MATCHING KNIVES AND WORK

The preceding pages have established the ground rules for knife design and construction and have explained how individual knife features contribute to a knife's function. The following pages offer specific recommendations—the patterns and relationships of blade to edge to tip to handle that are best suited to the diverse jobs assigned to modern knives.

Each type of knife is outlined by its primary characteristics: the steel that will perform best; the most practical blade length; the class of tip that blends best with function; whether the spine should be stiff, medium, or limber; the kind and the degree of bevel that should grace the blade and the edge; and the most practical kind of handle material.

My suggestions are not absolutes, but guidelines based on personal experience. If I suggest a straight carbon blade steel and you're in love with stainless, fine. That's what makes horse racing.

When I make more than one recommendation, the first listing is preferred; those that follow are acceptable in the order of their listing. For most food knives, for example, I prefer a Pakkawood handle, but I also recognize the comfortable heft and attractiveness that make wood an acceptable alternative.

Where illustration can be helpful, I've included a photo of a knife or knives representative of that class. The manufacturers of those knives are listed in the caption. When the name of the maker was not available, I've used the initials "NA."

The final listing is entitled "General Information." It is a collection of observations on the proper use, and occasional misuse, of that particular knife, along with a few explanations of the logic behind my recommendations.

Part II

Outdoor Knives

ALTHOUGH THE TERM "sporting knives" might be more appropriate than "outdoor knives" for this class of blade, I find it misleading. It either summons up images of what English gentlemen carry in their pockets to Epsom Downs, or of people walking around "sporting" knives—a scimitar, bolo knife, curved kris, or the like. This possibility isn't all that farfetched. I was once invited to a machete party. I attended out of curiosity and learned that it was a local bar's promotional scheme to introduce a pineapple-juice-and-vodka concoction called a machete. I learned nothing about knives but discovered a pretty good drink.

"Outdoor knives" seems a more accurate description, since this type of cutlery is used in outdoor pursuits, defense, and hobbies. There are a few generalizations that can be made about these knives as a class: they are heavy knives, characterized by sturdy construction, with tangs that reach through the handle. Also, they have thick, stiff-spined blades, and the steel from which they're fashioned is some of the hardest in the knife business, registering 58 to 60 on the Rockwell Scale.

The reason for such hardness is their status as a utility tool. Outdoor knives are expected to do many heavy jobs that would dull a lighter blade. They're also carried or worn, typically away from the home. It would be impractical to carry sharpening tools too, so, even though it takes some effort to hone these knives when you finally *are* near your tools, it's justified. They'll hold their edge for a long, long time.

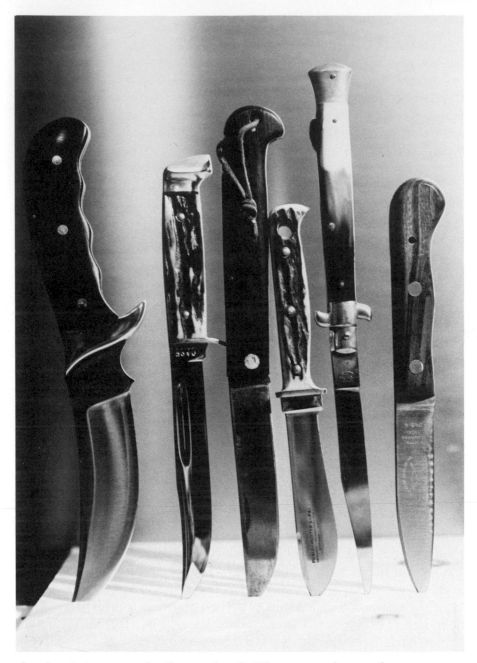

Outdoor knives are truly all-around tools. They are sturdy enough to stand up to heavy cutting chores, they hold a keen edge that doesn't require frequent sharpening, and they even function as a personal adornment. (Buck, Case, Kabar, Puma, Inax, E. A. Berg)

Of the various classes of knives, this one functions most often as a kind of personal adornment; consequently, their construction and conformation often follow, in some degree, artistic considerations. In fact, there's a flourishing business in the custom manufacture of outdoor knives. (With the exception of table carving sets, I know of no custom-made food or shop knives.) This notion of an outdoor knife as personal adornment has a negative aspect, too. Many sportsmen choose knives because they appeal to an overweening machismo—not because the particular design they choose will best do the job they plan for it.

Of all the outdoor knives, the big-game knife is subject to the wildest interpretations. This trio exhibits sensible design and tasteful construction that will prove their worth afield. (Morseth, Randall, Case)

I witnessed a full-blown example of the knife as a personal state-ment several years ago in a coffee shop on the New York State Thru-way. It was the wee hours of the opening day of deer season, and the knives displayed on the hips of the hunters drinking coffee there were a collector's delight. There was a plethora of huge bowie knives, and nearly as many bayonets. I saw one Arkansas toothpick and three sur-vival knives. One hunter had a throwing knife on his hip, but he left before I could ask him how he was planning to kill his deer. The dis-play was interesting too: all these mischosen knives were worn in a prominent place. If a hunter had a bowie and he wore a coat, he figured out how to get that knife *outside* the coat. One notable exception was a fellow who wore a car-length wool jacket—and carried the sheath holding his knife on a string tied to his belt, so that the sheath dangled down about midcalf.

There was, however, a small percentage of men who drank their coffee quietly and were revealed as hunters only by their checkered jackets. I assumed that they wore 4- to 6-inch big-game knives, close to their belts and under their jackets. There weren't many of them—maybe ten out of the hundred gathered there. The next day I read an interesting article about the opening of the deer season. It mentioned that hunter success in New York State runs about 10 percent every year.

HUNTING KNIVES

There is no generic term more misused than "hunting knife." It has come to be synonymous with any one-piece knife carried in a sheath. This is incorrect. Hunting knives are used in the taking, clean-ing, or skinning of game animals. The knife types fall into four categor-ies, each with specific design features that set them apart from other sheath knives.

The Big-Game Knife
Steel: Straight carbon or carbon alloy.
Length: Blade 4 to 7 inches, 8 to 11 inches overall.
Tip: Long clip, spear or rigging.
Spine: Stiff.
Blade bevel: Dropped V, V.
Edge bevel: Double edge, 24 to 30 degrees.
Handle: Pommel, guard, spacers. Material: Staghorn, leather, wood, synthetics.

General information: This knife is carried afield and is used to field-dress big-game animals, a procedure that involves the cutting of flesh and the splitting of soft bone.

Of all the outdoor knives, the big-game knife is subject to the wildest interpretations and most fanciful designs. Selecting a knife with too long a blade is the most common error. These knives are called on to make a wide variety of delicate tip cuts, and a long blade is difficult to control. For deer, a blade of 4 to 5 inches is sufficient. On larger big-game animals like elk and moose, you'll need a larger knife. In any event, I have never found the need for a big-game knife with a blade longer than 7 inches—and even that blade was suitable only for moose.

A big-game knife should have a hilt or guard to protect your fingers and hands when you are working inside the stomach cavity and to give you some extra leverage for the stab cuts you will have to make when cutting behind the esophagus and when fleshing out the anus.

A metal pommel is advisable to protect the handle from rearward blows. To properly clean big game, you must split the pelvic bone. To accomplish this, insert the tip of the knife into the soft part of the bone and drive it deeper by striking the knife butt with the palm of your hand or a rock.

During the cleaning process, a big-game knife is often used to pry bone apart. This necessitates a stiff, thick spine. So does another method of breaking the pelvis, useful on larger animals like elk: lay the edge of the knife along the pelvic joint and strike the back of the knife with a rock. This drives the edge into the cartilaginous bone, and it cleaves as efficiently (and more accurately) than does an ax.

The point on a big-game knife is second only to length in importance. Long, graceful points don't belong on this blade; they lack the strength for the prying work they must do, and they're easily broken.

Another poor choice is a scimitar point. When the knife point falls above the line of the knife back, the viscera are often punctured during the gutting process, which in turn spills the stomach contents over the meat and taints it. A scimitar point is difficult to control when you can't see it because it is out of line with the handle.

Choils can be useful on a hunting knife, since they promote delicate control. They are most practical on the back of the knife. When they are part of the cutting edge, especially on a short-bladed knife, they often interfere with clean slicing.

The Skinning Knife
Steel: Carbon alloy, stainless.
Length: Blade 4 to 6 inches, 8 to 10 inches overall.
Tip: Skinning.
Spine: Stiff or medium stiff.
Blade bevel: Dropped V, V grind, or concave grind.
Edge bevel: Double edge, 30 to 36 degrees.
Handle: Guard with short quillons. Material: Synthetic, staghorn, wood.
General information: There is some question about whether a skinning
      knife should be considered a hunting knife or a butcher knife. It
      is used to separate the hide from the flesh of big-game and domestic
      animals.

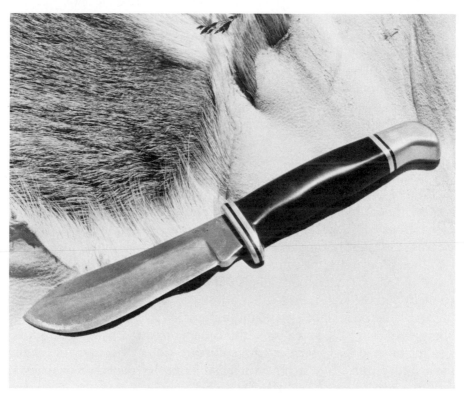

*In the skinning of big game, most of the work is done with one third
of the blade—the rounded leading edge near the tip. Hence, an extensive
tip area is one mark of a good skinner. Bluntish points are another good
idea, as piercing a hide ruins it for tanning. (Buck)*

Whatever its rightful class, the skinning knife is a far more specialized tool than the big-game knife. Its basic functions are tip slicing and wedging.

In the skinning process, the point of the knife is inserted between hide and skin. It doesn't really slice the two apart; it separates them. Once penetration is achieved, the easiest way to further separate hide from flesh is to wedge it apart by turning the knife sideways. When the subcutaneous membrane is too tough to give way to this pressure, the knife will cut this soft connecting material, but never hide or flesh.

The straight edge of the skinning blade is seldom used, as virtually all the cutting work is done at the rounded tip. A smooth wrist action works the blade in controlled semicircles, and once a section of the hide-to-flesh attachment is loosened, an equal amount of hide can usually be muscled free by pulling on it.

This unusual duty calls for a somewhat unusual design. Skinning is relatively precise work, so a short blade is the norm. Because the blade also functions as a wedge, it is deep in proportion to its length: a 2-inch-deep blade on a 5-inch knife demonstrates a good ratio.

During the skinning process great care must be taken not to slice the flesh or, worse yet, pierce the hide. A cut in a hide renders it nearly worthless. For this reason, the most practical skinners will have a blunt, almost rounded, point. There need only be enough of a point to find its way between hide and flesh.

The blunted point is also useful for working around legs. With a blunted point, you can run the tip from the animal's body to the first leg joint, slicing skin like a zipper in one straight cut. A scimitar-bladed skinning knife (of which there are many, though I don't know why) catches its pointy tip and cuts deep into leg meat when you try this.

Since all the slicing is done at the rounded forward end of the blade, this area should be extensive. Viewed in profile, the best skinning knives will have almost bulbous proportions near the tip.

The semicircles described by a skinning knife during the cutting process revolve on an axis near the handle. It is virtually all wrist work, and the cutting is done away from you. Because of this, it's important that the knife rest comfortably in your grip with your thumb either on top of the handle or on the back of the knife. It is the pressure of your thumb that will do most of the work. Guards are not an absolute requirement on a skinning knife, as they tend to interfere with penetration. If they are absent, however, the blade should have a choil to prevent your hand from sliding down on the sharpened edge. Choils are a good idea in any event, since they afford more control.

Because of frequent contact with hair, dirt, and meat, skinning knives should be washed often during the skinning process. For this reason, I prefer a synthetic handle, though I insist it have a nonslip surface. The fats you come in contact with while skinning are capable of making any smooth surface slick as ice, and unless you have a textured handle you'll have trouble holding onto the knife.

The Caping Knife

Steel: Straight carbon, carbon alloy, stainless.
Length: Blade 2½ to 3½ inches, 7 to 8 inches overall.
Tip: Skinning or rigging tip.
Spine: Medium stiff.
Blade bevel: V grind, hollow, or concave.
Edge bevel: Double edge, 18 to 24 degrees.
Handle: Guard, pommel optional. Material: Synthetic, staghorn, wood, leather.

Caping knives are mini-skinning knives used for delicate skinning jobs such as caping out big-game heads and preparing fowl capes, necks, and small-game skins for the fly-tying bench. Here a bucktail has been boned out and is ready for salting. (Buck)

General information: Caping knives fall somewhere between skinning knives and surgeon's scalpels. They are really taxidermy knives, used for caping out the delicate contours and the flimsy skin around the eyes, horns, mouth, and ears of big-game trophy heads.

Because this job requires precision, caping knives have short blades, 2½ to 3½ inches long. Although they're small, they are still a kind of skinning knife, so at least one of the skinner's features carries over—a relatively broad point close to the level of the back. They are not wide in profile like the skinner, since they must twist and turn to flesh out tight contours and fit into narrow crannies. They are also sharpened to a shaving edge. The skin-to-bone attachments around the head are much more leathery than those on the carcass.

The one feature I have found consistently disappointing in knives that would otherwise make fine capers is the length of their handles. Perhaps out of some unjustified sense of visual balance, many of these short blades come attached to short handles that refuse to fit comfortably in your hand. This makes precise blade work more difficult.

Because a caper is never used for hammering or wedging bone, this is one outdoor knife that could sensibly incorporate a hollow-ground edge for ease in sharpening.

The caping knife is used much like the skinning knife, with the tip coming into play most often. The knife swings in tight semicircles to cut the hide free. The caping process, like the knife, is scaled down, though. A skinner's sweep may cover a foot; a caper's stroke is measured in inches at the most.

The Bird Knife
Steel: Straight carbon, carbon alloy, stainless alloy.
Length: Blade 2½ to 3½ inches, 7 to 8 inches overall.
Tip: Long clip, spear or rigging.
Spine: Stiff or medium stiff.
Blade bevel: V grind or dropped V.
Edge bevel: 30 to 36 degrees.
Handle: Guard, pommel optional. Material: Synthetic, staghorn, wood, leather.
General information: Bird knives are brothers to caping knives—but not twins. They are short bladed not so much for control as for safety. Birds are most easily cleaned in your hand, and a long-bladed knife could easily pass through the carcass and into your palm.

Birds are most easily cleaned in one's hand, so a short blade ensures against cuts. A bird knife is also called on to cleave light bone and therefore requires a stiff blade and a strong edge. (Ontario Knife Co.)

It is easiest to clean the bird after it has been plucked. You get a clearer view of what you're doing; and, if you reverse the process, blood and viscera mat the feathers in the area of the vent and this makes plucking more difficult.

To remove the entrails, open the stomach cavity from the vent to the end of the breastbone and scoop them out with your hand. The feet, wings, and neck are a little more difficult.

The feet are severed at the joint immediately below the drumstick. Cut the cartilage cleanly at the exact point of hinging.

Wings are usually plucked up to the first joint. Bend the wing backward and cut at the point of hinging, from the inside of the joint out. You will probably have to make several cuts, as this joint is connected by tough sinew, and you may have to do some delicate teasing work with the tip—another reason for a small blade.

Except on the smallest of game birds, like doves and quail, the head can't be cut free with a smooth stroke of the blade. The bone is too tough. Lay the bird on a cutting board with the edge of the knife across its neck. Press the blade point down firmly with the fingers of your left hand (if you're right-handed). The edge should now be at an approximate 45-degree angle to the board. Bring the handle down sharply, like a paper cutter, keeping pressure on the tip, and you'll cleave through the neck bone.

On larger birds, like geese and turkeys, you'll have to use this procedure on the legs, and you may have to use a cleaver on the neck. In the absence of a cleaver, you can lay the bird knife in position and strike the spine with a hammer or rock. Because of this hard use, you're wisest to choose a bird knife with a broad spine and a strong edge. These two characteristics of blade design are what separate true bird knives from true caping knives.

Folding Hunting Knives

Folding hunting knives have always been popular among a small segment of the sporting public, but the last decade has seen their manufacture and use increase markedly.

Folding big-game knives must be strong; consequently, they should have no more than one blade. Blade dimensions and conformation approximate those features that make a top-notch one-piece big-game knife. (Case, Buck)

I have a hunch that the same pride of possession and determination to have a one-of-a-kind knife that drives some of us to buy custom one-piece knives is responsible for the sudden popularity of the folding hunter. When you examine their debits and credits, they don't make much sense in any other light.

My main doubt regarding folders for hunting lies in their inherent weakness. No matter how good the quality of the steel, or how sturdy their rivets, pivots, and locks, a ten-or-more-piece knife can never be as strong and durable as the solid blade-and-tang of one-piece construction.

The advantages of a folding knife all lie in the fact that they can be carried in one's pocket, but even the 3-inch blade of a caping or bird knife requires a large package to house its blade. When I walk for several miles, I find that package irritating in my pocket, a heavy burden that rubs denim or wool against my thigh like sandpaper. Larger knives, capable of gutting big game, are proportionately more intolerable.

These larger folding knives can be carried in a sheath, but if you're going to carry your blade on your belt, why not use a one-piece knife in the first place?

Cleanliness is another factor. Folding knives around any food material become catchalls that defy cleaning, and meat and fat gum their joints.

Still, the folding knife's popularity for hunting persists. If it appeals to you, here are a few things to look for:

• Big-game folders should conform to the guidelines laid down for one-piece big-game knives. They should be single-bladed knives, since this makes for the strongest construction, and they should have a locking device to keep them from closing on your hand.

• Folding skinning knives are really folding caping knives. For most of us, there is no justification for a folding big-game skinner, since game (or domestic livestock) is seldom skinned in the field. A big folding skinner in your pocket would amount to a useless burden. Trappers, however, often have need of a caping-class folding knife for skinning small- to medium-sized furbearers like muskrat, weasel, and beaver. A 3- or 4-inch, V-ground blade with a needle tip is the preferred cutting tool. Trappers I have spoken to prefer an opposing double-bladed folder with identical blades on each end of the knife.

• Bird knives that can be carried in your pocket make the most

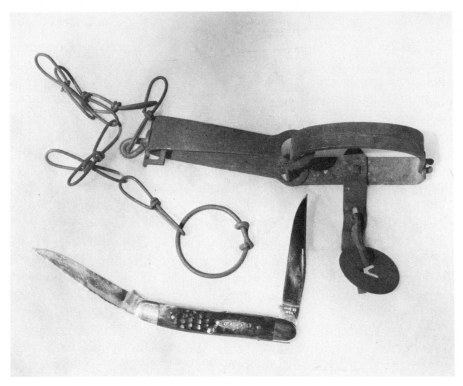

This folding-knife pattern, appropriately called "the muskrat," is a favorite among professional trappers. (Case)

sense of all the folding hunters. To me, a folding knife has always amounted to "pocket stuff"—an important part of the assorted tools that I carry with me every day. When I go bird hunting, I seldom remember to strap on a sheath knife. Thus, I've cleaned a lot more birds with a folder than with my carefully selected bird knife.

Again, follow the guidelines laid down for one-piece bird knives. I don't think that the limitations imposed on general utility by a single-bladed knife are justified by the job a bird knife is expected to do. They don't have to be as strong laterally as a big-game knife; consequently, my "pocket stuff" knife has seven blades. Think twice, however, before you strike the spine of a folder with a rock. Folders won't take that much punishment.

Hunting Blade Variations

Humans have a universal commitment to building a better mousetrap, a commitment which is evident in knives as in everything else.

You often run across big-game knives with radically upswept tips, the idea being that the blade will double as big-game knife and skinner. It's an admirable idea, but it doesn't pan out in practice. The sharp point required for stab cuts too often snags and ruins hide. The extensive curved leading-edge area of the tip needed for skinning throws the point out of control—and you cut viscera. When dealing with tools, I have found that using the one designed for the specific job turns in a far better performance than a jack-of-all-trades that, in truth, is the master of none.

The same may be said of a few other experiments with the basic hunting blade.

• Gutting notches or gutting hooks are a crescent of steel ground out of the blade. The crescent is sharpened on the inside of the curve. Its intended function is to hook into a small incision in the stomach cavity of big game, then slice it open like a zipper without cutting into viscera.

I have tried gutting notches of several designs. Unless they are incorporated into a gutting-notch blade whose exclusive purpose is opening the stomach cavity, I find them flawed because they are never of sufficient depth to do the job for which they were intended. Too, they don't span the area from outside skin to internal cavity, and, as a result they don't cut properly. They are also difficult to sharpen correctly, and as you use them they cut free a great amount of hair—which invariably ends up on the meat. Belly hair on wild meat is a common cause of a so-called "gamy" taste. There is only one way to properly lay open a stomach cavity once the initial incision has been made, and that is by cutting from the inside out with a sharp, straight edge.

• Sawteeth on the back of a blade are supposed to cut through bone, a necessity when a big-game animal must be quartered and packed out in the wilderness. The number of teeth that can be machined into a 4-to-7-inch blade will never be sufficient to cut bone cleanly, and the ⅛-to-³⁄₁₆-inch-wide back of a proper hunting knife cuts too wide a swath for practical sawing. I've labored for half an hour over a single leg bone with a saw-backed knife and have come to the conclusion that a small, light meat saw makes much more sense.

• Sharpened swedges are downright dangerous. They represent a mistaken crossover from the combat and survival class of knives, and serve no purpose on a hunting knife.

One example of inventiveness in outdoor knife design is the Skachet.
It incorporates a gutting notch, a knife edge and skinner tip, and a hammer
head on the opposing side of the blade. In addition, the knife has a
threaded 1-inch hole in the handle into which you can twist a sturdy, straight
branch, making the Skachet a hatchet.

FISHING KNIVES

The work cut out for fishing knives always involves water, so they are commonly made of stainless steel or a stainless alloy. Fish flesh and bones are soft compared to the bones of birds and big game, and the work these knives do seldom involves chopping or prying, so fishing knives are generally lighter in appearance and construction than hunting knives are.

Although some fishing knives resemble filet knives, this kind of compromise in design never works out. True fishing knives make poor filet knives and vice versa. (See "Filet Knives" under "Seafood," page 141.)

Handling fish will involve slime, so the handle on a fish knife should be unusually rough and pebbly. Because fishing knives are used primarily in and around water, one of the many synthetic handle materials is best. The most positive grip I have run across is a rubbery plastic with a finish like coarse-grit sandpaper. Guards and pommels are generally not required on a fishing knife.

Saltwater Fishing Knife
Steel: Stainless or stainless alloy.
Length: Blade 4 to 8 inches, 8 to 12 inches overall.
Tip: Long clip or rigging.
Spine: Medium.
Blade bevel: V grind, hollow, or concave grind.
Edge bevel: Double edge, 21 to 27 degrees.
Handle: Synthetic or cork.
General information: The saltwater fishing knife is used to gut and trim
    fish, cut lines, and prepare bait (though a bait knife does this job
    better). One of the saltwater fishing knife's most important duties
    will be cutting hooks from the mouths of fish. Often baits or lures
    are deeply ingested, so when you're dealing with large fish a long
    blade helps keep your fingers away from their toothy mouths.
    Large fish (20 pounds and up) also have strong enough backbones
to warrant a V grind rather than a hollow grind. You often have to
lever or chop through the backbone when trimming the head and
tail. (This procedure is listed under bird knives.)
    A cork handle provides a solid grip under the slimiest of conditions, and it keeps the knife afloat should you drop it overboard. It is
not a particularly durable handle, however.

A typical knife for large saltwater game fish. The stainless blade is long enough to cut deeply ingested hooks free and to clean big stripers and salmon. The spoon at the knife butt is used to scoop out entrails and the blood vein that lies against a fish's backbone. (Ontario Knife Co.)

While you may want to carry these knives in a sheath when you're fishing, don't store them there between trips. Even the best stainless steel can corrode under the combined assault of heat, moisture, and salt. They are best stored in a rack—and most prone to corrosion when stored sheathed in a tackle box.

Freshwater Fishing Knife
Steel: Stainless or stainless alloy.
Length: Blade 3 to 6 inches, 7 to 10 inches overall.
Tip: Long clip or rigging.
Spine: Medium.
Blade bevel: V grind, hollow, or concave grind.
Edge bevel: Double edge, 21 to 27 degrees.
Handle: Synthetic or cork.
General information: Since fresh water is not nearly so corrosive as salt water, you can choose a straight carbon or carbon alloy blade for this knife if you prefer. You will, however, have to mother the blade a bit: any moisture will eventually cause rust.

The larger freshwater fish, like pike and lake trout, necessitate long blades. Smaller fish, like trout, can be trimmed and cleaned with a 3-inch blade. Since you hold smaller fish in your hand to clean them, short blades are also advisable from a safety standpoint.

Larger freshwater species such as pike and lake trout are best cleaned with a sheath knife. Note that virtually all fish knives share features with filet knives. This model also has a serrated back for scaling. (Queen)

Bait Knife

Steel: Stainless or stainless alloy.
Length: Blade 3 to 4 inches, 7 to 8 inches overall.
Tip: Spear, rigging, clip.
Spine: Medium stiff.
Blade bevel: V grind.
Edge bevel: Double edge, 24 to 30 degrees.
Handle: Synthetic, cork, wood.
General information: The bait knife is used to prepare and rig bait like mullet, menhaden, squid, and shrimp. It is more of a slicing

than a penetrating knife; hence it is deeper in profile than a fish knife and has a spear point.

A sawtooth back on a bait knife is advisable, since it will enable you to cut frozen bait. These teeth work best when they're spaced

Bait knives are called on to do a wide variety of cutting work around salt water. A sawtooth back facilitates cutting frozen bait, functions as a scaler, and will cut through soft fish bone. (G&C, under jig; NA, NA, NA, NA)

wider apart than the close teeth of a meat saw; it is roughly a compromise between a meat saw and a scalloped edge. The sawteeth can also be used to scale fish and to cut through thick fishbone.

Folding Fishing Knives

Because lateral strength is not a major concern in a fishing knife, folders are a practical alternative to a one-piece knife—under certain conditions.

The long blades needed to deal with the larger fish preclude folders from this category; there is no sense in carrying a 6-inch (or larger) knife in your pocket. Salt water is another limiting factor. A folder regularly used around salt water will get clogged with gunk and corrode, no matter what type of steel is used in its construction.

Folders are largely limited to use around fresh water, but in that milieu two designs stand out.

The Fish Knife
Steel: Stainless or stainless alloy.
Length: Blades 3½ to 4 inches, 5 inches closed.
Tip: Long clip on master blade, hook disgorger on supplementary blade.
Spine: Stiff.
Blade bevel: V grind.
Edge bevel: Double edge, 24 to 30 degrees.
Handle: Synthetic, wood, or bone.

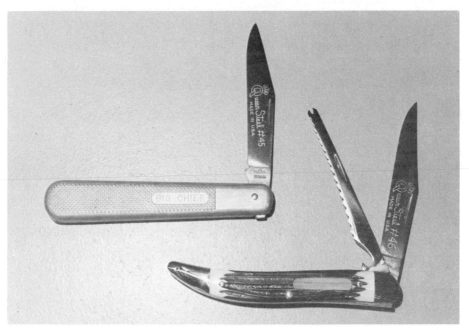

The fish knife is a standard folder pattern that includes a master blade and a scaling/hook-disgorger blade. The single-bladed folder on the right makes a fine knife for gutting and trimming most freshwater fish, and may be used around salt water since it's made entirely of stainless steel. (Queen, Queen)

General information: The "fish knife" is a standard design in pocket-knife manufacture. The master blade is large enough to deal with the requirements for pike, bass, walleye, and other large fresh-water game fish. The supplementary blade has a hook disgorger at the tip and an edge that functions as a scaler and saw. This blade often incorporates a bottle opener too. Another handy feature some-times included with this knife is a hook honer imbedded in the handle.

The Swiss Army Knife
Steel: Stainless alloy.
Length: Blades 1½ to 3 inches, 2½ to 3½ inches closed.
Tip: Master blade, spear. Supplementary blades: Clip, scissors, screw-driver, file, ad infinitum.
Spine: Stiff.

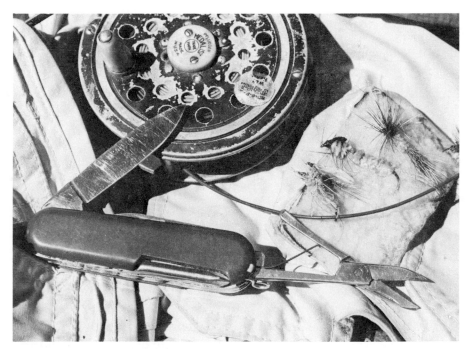

One of the many blades available with the Swiss Army Folder is a pair of small scissors. Add a small spear blade and you have the perfect knife for a trout fisherman; it will trim leader, clip hackle, cut reluctant hooks free, and clean the fish you wish to creel. (Precise Imports Corp.)

Blade bevel: V grind.

Edge bevel: Double edge, 21 to 27 degrees.

Handle: Synthetic.

General information: The Swiss army knife is a multibladed pocket-knife that's extremely popular with hikers and campers. The knife comes in more than a dozen models, with a wide variety of blade designs and blade combinations available. It is an excellent knife for the trout fisherman because the spear and clip blades are more than sufficient for cleaning these fish. The scissors incorporated into the knife are ideal for cutting the tab end of a leader off a knotted hook eye and for trimming flies.

DIVING KNIVES

Knives designed for skin and scuba diving are a class unto themselves. They are massive knives constructed from materials that will not be affected by constant submersion. Their appearance, design, and function were best summed up by a friend whom I had asked to tell me all he knew about diving knives. He began by saying, "Well, they're not exactly a knife; they're more like a cross between a sledgehammer and a crowbar with a sharpened edge. . . ."

The Diving Knife

Steel: Stainless with a high nickel content.

Length: Blade 5 to 8 inches, 9 to 13 inches overall.

Tip: Spear or clip, often with a sharpened swedge.

Spine: Stiff and massive; often ¼ inch wide with sawteeth.

Blade bevel: Dropped V.

Edge bevel: Double-edge or cannel, 36 to 42 degrees. Sharpened swedge, if present, 45 to 51 degrees.

Handle: Rubber or soft plastic. Large guard, massive, heavy pommel, usually flat so it can be used as a hammer.

General information: Nickel stainless steel is the most corrosion resistant of all stainless alloys, and it has high impact resistance as well. A virtually indestructible blade is needed in a diving knife.

A particularly sharp edge is not really that important—clean cutting is not one of the major jobs for this knife. For the most part, it is used like a pry bar: to break free samples of coral or abalone, or as a shovel to dig clams from the sand.

Indestructible is the quality that best describes diving knives. The center knife has an interesting safety feature: a pebbly gray blade finish that won't reflect light that could conceivably tempt a predatory fish into striking. (Puma, Dacor, Kabar, U.S. Divers, U.S. Divers)

The tip should be so low that it's in line with the handle; this gives maximum thrust control. It should also be rather blunt. This is one knife where a sharpened swedge or false edge makes sense, since it enhances the knife's ability to pry and cut rock-clinging shellfish lose. Sawteeth on the back of the blade is another worthwhile design feature. These teeth will cut through rope and vegetation more efficiently than a straight edge, because becoming entangled with lines or plants underwater is a far more likely danger than hand-to-hand combat with sharks.

Guards and a large pommel belong on a skin-diving knife. The pommel can be used as a hammer. The handle should also have a wrist thong so you can use your hands without having to sheath the knife or lay it down.

Handle material must be some sort of synthetic, since no other handle material (short of solid steel) will take constant immersion.

Plastic is a plus, too, in that it can be cast with air bubbles inside to achieve near-neutral buoyancy when the knife is underwater. This kind of handle makes the knife sink very slowly, so it's easy to retrieve should you drop it. It's also easier to work with than a heavy knife or a knife with a floating handle. These floating handles may seem like a good idea underwater, but they'll drive you mad. You never expect things to fall up, and floating knives are forever drifting out of your grasp.

Sheaths for skin-diving knives, too, should be made of some synthetic with a positive locking device to hold the knife in place. The simplest and most effective lock I have run across is a peg on the sheath that fits into a hole in the handle of the knife. Once the strap and clasp are snapped in place, it is impossible for the knife to work free. Skin-diving sheaths should be constructed in such a way that they can be worn on your leg.

CAMPING KNIVES

Like living at home, camping may require a multiplicity of edges for cooking and outdoor work. The type of knife you'll need depends on the type of camping you'll be doing.

If you're camping in a large recreational vehicle, there's no reason why you can't carry a full complement of kitchen and sporting knives. In fact, when I take my recvee antelope hunting on the hot plains, I bring along my butcher tools as well so I can package the meat and get it into a cooler before the warm temperatures spoil the carcass.

When you're car camping with a tent or traveling with a recreational vehicle, I would recommend that you bring at least four knives for cooking: a paring knife, a utility knife, a meat-slicing knife, and a French chef's knife (see "Food Knives," page 115). You'll also have room for whatever sporting knives you'll need for your outdoor activities.

You will have to limit your selection more carefully, however, if your camping tastes run to backpacking. Backpacking requires carrying your home on your back. It is spare sport whose success is measured by the degree of economy you engineer into your selection of gear. "Light" and "multipurpose" are the bywords of backpacking, so the knives you carry should be chosen with all-around utility in mind.

Camping Sheath Knife
Steel: Straight carbon, carbon alloy.
Length: Blade 3 to 5 inches, 6 to 9 inches overall.
Tip: Spear or rigging.
Spinc: Medium stiff.
Blade bevel: V-grind.
Edge bevel: Double edge, 24 to 30 degrees.
Handle: Synthetic, Pakkawood, staghorn, or leather.
General information: A sheath knife for camping will be most useful for preparing foods. In this capacity, its most common use will be as a slicer, parer, and dicer, so a thin V-grind blade with a deep profile is recommended.

The spare lines of this light sheath knife make it an excellent companion on a backpack trip. The "Tinker" pattern of the Swiss Army Knife folder packs six extremely useful blades into a light frame. It is capable of innumerable, and invaluable, repair jobs in the wilderness. (E. A. Berg, Precise Imports Corp.)

Such a knife, so long as it has a medium-stiff spine, is also capable of many other camp jobs: whittling forked sticks for cooking, sharpening pegs for tents, cleaning fish and even cleaning large and small game. It will do none of these jobs as well as the special blade designed for each task, however.

Although the camp knife may be pressed into heavy duty at times, guards and pommels are not advisable since they interfere with many of the other tasks this blade will be expected to perform. Since you will sometimes use it to prepare food, look for handle material and an overall design that can be easily cleaned.

While the one-piece camping knife is designed to be carried on your belt, it is usually most comfortable to tuck the sheathed knife inside your pack. The pack frame and waistband make wearing them on your belt impractical and uncomfortable.

Folding Camping Knives
Steel: Straight carbon, carbon alloy, stainless, stainless alloy.
Length: Master blade, 2 to 3 inches. Overall, 3 to 3½ inches.
Tip: Master blade, spear. Supplementary blades: Screwdriver, sheep foot, clip, can opener, awl, file, ad infinitum.
Spine: Stiff.
Blade bevel: V-grind.
Edge bevel: Master: double edge, 24 to 30 degrees. Clip: double edge, 18 to 24 degrees. Awl: single edge, 45 degrees.
Handle: Synthetic, staghorn, wood.
General information: The granddaddy of the folding camp knife is the durable Boy Scout knife, a design that has survived because of its practicality. This knife and some of its more modern counterparts are truly worth their weight in gold around camp, for they pack into one small, light frame the ability to do so many jobs.

Another folding camper worthy of note is the Swiss Army Knife. This knife comes in an incredible number of models with dozens of blades, including things like magnifying glasses, spoons, saws, and corkscrews. In all candor, I think these twelve- to twenty-four-bladed knives are a little silly—you'll never get to use half the blades you could conceivably pack into the handle, and they make the knife that much heavier and bulkier in your pocket.

I do think, however, that the six- to ten-bladed knives can be fine examples of functional design, and one model, the "Tinker," has suited my needs for over ten years. Some of the jobs this knife has done over and above prosaic camp chores provide ample testimony to its usefulness.

• The awl helped me to sew one of my pack's straps together temporarily after an alpine-dwelling rodent called a coney chewed it in half one night in its hunger for salt.

• The standard-bit screwdrivers have tightened scope mounts on my rifle, have undone and helped repair malfunctioning reels on the shores of glacial lakes, have pried loose swelled cartridges in gun chambers, and have proved essential to many repairs on pack frames.

• The Phillips head screwdriver once tightened the base of a compass that was reading incorrectly because of vibrations. The compass was on a float plane taking me out of a fly-in camp 300 miles south of the Arctic Circle on a foggy, stormy day.

• The file has sharpened fishhooks, has smoothed the burred heads of screws that would otherwise have been impossible to tighten, and has polished an outboard motor part without which the motor would not have run the 10 miles over open water back to the safety of camp.

Add these unusual duties to things like opening cans and bottles and preparing food and you'll see that a small utility camping knife amounts to a big help indeed. I have learned the value of carrying one everywhere I go, camping or not.

Other Camp Cutting Tools

The hatchet and Hudson Bay ax are traditional cutting tools that come to mind whenever camping is mentioned, though nowadays their usefulness is debatable.

Their original popularity stemmed from the fact that they epitomized utility. If you knew how to handle them properly, you could literally build a house—including the furnishings inside—with them. But the days of log trapper's cabins and tent poles cut from the forest are long gone. They have been replaced by an era of nylon tents, aluminum pegs, and Ensolite groundcloths. About the only practical use these tools now have around camp is chopping firewood, and they're surpassed at this job by folding "swede" saws that eat through wood with less effort and are safer to use.

THE KNIFE AS WEAPON

One of the many functions of the knife throughout the course of history has been as an instrument of offense and defense. A knife designed primarily as a weapon shares three traits: unusual blade length, unusual blade thickness, and a sharpened swedge.

• A long blade serves to keep some distance between you and your opponent. Classic fighting knives have a blade between 8 and 12 inches long and a large guard with long quillons to protect the user's hand.

• Blades are thick for lateral strength. A strong, unbending spine is needed to deflect thrusts and blows from the blade of an opponent and to keep one's thrusts from being deflected or bent aside. A broken blade in a pitched battle could be deadly, so some variation of the strong V-grind blade bevel is usually part of a combat knife's design.

Another adaptation for strength in a fighting blade is the so-called "blood groove." It's commonly thought that this long, dished indentation in a knife blade was designed to allow easy removal of the blade after it had deeply penetrated flesh, but in fact this groove was designed to strengthen the blade by creating more surface area and, thus, greater resistance to stress.

• A sharpened swedge allows easy penetration. As the point drives deeper, the two edges separate and cut flesh. On the same principle, knives used exclusively for fighting have a point in line with the handle for maximum thrusting power.

Perhaps because of our fear and fascination hangups with instruments of violence, many of the old fighting designs are still prominent today. I see all too many knives with combat features used as hunting, fishing, and camping knives, and I can think of no kind words for the manufacturers who choose this design for such work. It is simply ignorant—and it can be dangerous as well. With this in mind, remember the features of fighting knives so you aren't handicapped by a weapon when you actually need a working knife.

The Stiletto
Steel: Straight carbon.
Length: Blade 6 to 9 inches, 12 inches overall.
Tip: Needle point, extremely slender.

Blade bevel: Triangular or quadrangular blade, extremely slender in profile. Unsharpened edge.

Handle: Silver, jewels, staghorn. Graceful guard with long quillons.

General information: Historically, the stiletto was an Italian knife used for personal defense in the seventeenth century. It was a sheath-type dagger designed for puncturing, not cutting.

Arkansas Toothpick

Steel: Straight carbon.

Length: Blade 8 to 12 inches, 12 to 16 inches overall.

Tip: Slender spear.

Spine: Stiff, running down the center of the blade.

Blade bevel: Double V grind. This knife was sharpened on both edges.

Edge bevel: 30 to 36 degrees.

Handle: Leather, wood, staghorn; large guard, long quillons and pommel.

General information: The Arkansas toothpick was a dagger used by American frontiersmen. The blade was double-edged for its full length, but the bevel was acute enough to be honed to a rather fine edge. It could function as a cutting tool, but its primary function was still defense—as is evidenced by that double edge, its 10-inch blade, and a point in line with the handle.

The Bowie Knife

Steel: Historically, straight carbon. Currently, carbon or stainless alloy.

Length: Blade 10 to 12 inches, 14 to 16 inches overall.

Tip: Saber or clip with sharpened swedge.

Spine: Stiff, with thickest part of blade between back and edge.

Blade bevel: Dropped V or a rounded variation of the dropped V. Viewed cross-sectionally, some bowies look like a narrow oval.

Edge bevel: 24 to 30 degrees, double-edge on both edge and swedge. Occasionally cannel.

Handle: Leather, wood, staghorn. Large guard, massive pommel. The heavy handle on a bowie could be used like a club as a supplementary weapon.

General information: The bowie knife represents frontier ingenuity at its best. Although Jim Bowie popularized this knife, credit for the basic design belongs to his brother, Rezin. While knives were an important weapon of self-defense in the early 1800s, Rezin Bowie

*The bowie knife is an all-American design that was perfectly suited to
life on the frontier. Of special note is the brass sleeve, which snaps over the
unsharpened knife back, a device that caught and held an opponent's blade.
The incredible versatility of the bowie is no longer needed today, yet with
a few modifications the design lives on in the modern big-game knife. (Case)*

perceived their utilitarian nature. Therefore, he altered the Arkansas
toothpick with work as well as protection in mind.

Bowie knives are big: a 10-inch blade is the standard. The point
is in line with the handle for powerful thrusting, the guard has long
quillons for hand protection, and the back of the knife has a swedge.
Up until the development of the bowie knife, swedges were unheard of.
The advantage of a swedge was that the user could cut an opponent on
an upstroke, yet still pressure and direct the knife from all but the last
third of the knife back without slicing his thumb or hand.

The strong, thick spine of the knife lay close to the back, enabling
a more acute blade bevel than was the case with the Arkansas toothpick. The cutting edge, slung well beneath the handle, could therefore
be honed to shaving sharpness, an advantage when the knife was to be
used as a tool or a weapon. The bowie handle was also designed so that the
knife could be comfortably held with the cutting edge up or down—another advantage when fighting or working.

Another ingenious adaptation was a brass sleeve that snapped over the unsharpened back of the knife. When a person parried with a bowie knife, warding off his opponent's thrust with the back of the blade, the soft brass caught and momentarily held his opponent's knife. A steel-backed knife merely deflected such a thrust, and the wild blade was thus still dangerous.

All in all, the bowie was like a third hand to the frontiersmen and mountain men who carried their worldly belongings in saddlebags and around their belts. It could chop, shape, and carve small trees for shelter and rudimentary tools, yet it was still capable of reasonably fine cutting, from skinning out a grizzly bear to slicing up a haunch of venison. And it was eminently useful for self-defense.

Frontier conditions don't prevail today, and neither does the need for a bowie knife; yet, in a way, the design still lives—though it has changed with evolution. Remove those features that lent themselves to fighting—the 4 inches of length, the brass sleeve, the sharpened swedge, and the large guard—and you have the basic big-game knife design, as practical today as the bowie was then.

The Bayonet

Steel: Straight carbon or carbon alloy.

Length: Blade 10 to 24 inches, 14 to 28 inches overall.

Tip: Slender spear, often with sharpened swedge.

Spine: Stiff.

Blade bevel: Radically dropped V below blood groove.

Edge bevel: 40 to 50 degrees, double edge.

Handle: Leather, synthetic. Pommel and guard adapted to lock onto the barrel of a rifle.

General information: The bayonet is the most common type of modern fighting knife, and it makes an interesting study in contrasts when compared to the bowie. A bayonet could aptly be described as a bowie knife with the fighting characteristics retained and the utility characteristics deemphasized—almost the opposite of a big-game knife.

Bayonets have large guards, a long blade, and an in-line point with a swedge. They are thick-spined, with a blood groove for strength, but they lack depth when viewed from the side—thereby sacrificing an acute bevel and, as a result, a sharp cutting edge. Their main function is killing, not cutting.

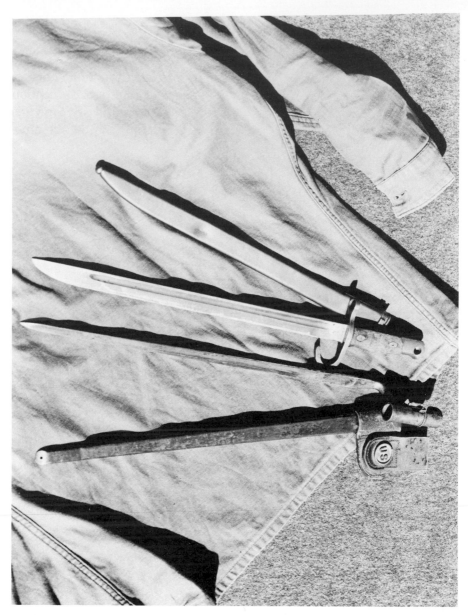

Although these two bayonets appear radically different, they are quite similar in principles of knife design. The slender Civil War bayonet has stilettolike lines with a triangular blade for strength and no cutting edge. The early World War II bayonet on the top is nearly as long, with an extremely slender profile and a blood groove for added strength. Although it has a sharpened edge, the blade bevel is too abrupt for fine cutting. Both knives are designed for deep point penetration—killing, not cutting.

Folding Fighting Knives

The inherent weakness of a folding knife makes it impractical as a weapon. A thrust that is the slightest bit out of line puts tremendous pressure on the bolster, as does any sort of powerful slash. However, the principles of the fighting knife are incorporated into one common folder, the contemporary stiletto.

The Folding Stiletto
Steel: Stainless or stainless alloy.
Length: 6 to 10 inches, 7 to 12 inches overall.
Tip: Slender spear with sharpened swedge.
Spine: Stiff.
Blade bevel: Radically dropped V. Blade extremely slender in profile.
Edge bevel: 40 to 50 degrees.
Handle: Synthetic, horn. Pommel and guard.
General information: The folding stiletto has an unusually thick-spined blade, with a point in line with the handle. Most of these knives also incorporate a locking device.

The folding stiletto is a dysfunctional knife by every measurement: too weak for combat, too unwieldy and dull for work, and too large to be carried comfortably. Because it has long been a favorite tool of criminals and punks, its manufacture and sale have been banned in most states. (Romo, Inax)

Many such folders are spring-loaded—"push-button" or "switch-blade" are common terms. They fly into the open position when you release the lock that holds them closed, usually by pressing a button in the handle.

Although the folding stiletto is a pocketknife, the features of its design define it as a weapon rather than a tool. It is nearly useless for cutting work, since its radical bevel can't be sharpened beyond 35 to 40 degrees. Because of its use as an offensive weapon, this knife is classed along with guns and dangerous weapons, and its possession is illegal in many states.

SURVIVAL KNIVES

Survival knives are another variation of design that falls somewhere between combat and outdoor knives. This class of knife is designed to suit the needs of men marooned in the wilderness or in hostile environments like enemy territory. They are standard equipment for clandestine military units such as rangers and frogmen and were part of the gear issued to U-2 pilots. More recently, specially designed survival knives were carried aloft during space exploration.

The Service Knife
Steel: Straight carbon or carbon alloy.
Length: Blade 6 to 8 inches, 10 to 12 inches overall.
Tip: Clip with swedge, sometimes sharpened.
Spine: Stiff and heavy.
Blade bevel: Dropped V, blade deep, usually with blood groove.
Edge bevel: 24 to 30 degrees, double edge.
Handle: Leather or synthetic. Large guard, heavy pommel.
General information: The service knife is typical of survival knives in
    that it combines the features of both utility knives and fighting
    knives. Its long blade, swedge, clublike pommel, and point in line
    with the handle reveal its use as a weapon. Its clip tip, strong
    blade, and edge that can be honed to shaving sharpness indicate
    general cutting and all-around function.

The service knife comes in many varieties of design, depending on the branch of the service that issued the knife and its date of manufacture, but the principles of this type of knife remain the same. Of all so-called "war surplus" knives, this one is the best big-game knife,

The principles of service knives remain the same, so this knife design has changed little over the years. The knife at the top is a U.S. Navy veteran of Vietnam. The bottom knife was issued to fliers in World War II.

though it is inferior to the blades specifically designed for that purpose. These blades usually have a blued finish so they don't reflect light and thereby reveal a soldier's location to an enemy.

Survival Knife
Steel: Straight carbon, carbon alloy, stainless, stainless alloy.
Length: Blade 6 to 8 inches, 10 to 12 inches overall.
Tip: Spear with swedge, usually sharpened.
Spine: Stiff, running down the middle of the blade profile; occasionally sawteeth on knife back.
Blade bevel: Dropped V.
Edge bevel: 24 to 36 degrees, double edge.
Handle: Synthetic, horn, or leather. Pommel and guard. On some knives the pommel screws in place and caps a waterproof hollow handle that can be used to carry fishhooks and line, medicine, matches, etc.
General information: Many aspects of the survival knife are reminiscent

of the bowie. The purpose of these knives is to provide a measure of defense as well as to work as a tool. They are shorter in blade than the bowie, since concealment and compactness are considerations, but they are wide-spined with a swedge, a point in line with the handle, and a double-eared guard. They are also capable of being honed to shaving sharpness, and they have a handle that fits the palm comfortably in any position.

The most notable improvement over the bowie designs is a hollow, waterproof handle, large enough to hold matches, fishline and hooks, medical supplies, and other small items necessary to survival. They're interesting conversation pieces and would surely be invaluable if you ever parachuted down in the jungles of Southeast Asia or in the Arctic tundra—and I feel that they're best suited to just those two types of situations. There are too many jobs expected of a survival knife for it to do any one job well—except, of course, to help you survive. Luckily most of us won't ever have to put them into practical use, no matter how vigorous our outdoor pursuits.

This most modern example of a survival knife is standard issue for U.S. astronauts. The edge is shaving sharp, the back of the blade is capable of sawing wood, and the blade is strong enough to be used as a pry. In addition, special lightweight steel and odorless polypropylene were used in blade and handle to fulfill two primary requirements of space flight: air purity and light weight. (Case)

THROWING KNIVES

Throwing knives constitute the most damn-foolish class of blades ever devised by man. For starters, they can't cut anything. As a fighting knife they're middling at best because they have no guard and their wide blade does not penetrate easily—and for finishers, the one unbreakable rule in hand combat is, "*Never* throw your weapon away."

Still, I'll be the first to admit a childish fascination in the ability to tattoo a wood board with whirling, flashing blades. This type of pleasure is related to that of a game of genteel darts, to the grace of archery, and to the power and accuracy of a 300-yard bullet that hits the bulls-eye; and all these elements seem to be present in the comfortable thunk of a blade thrown true. So this class of knives survives and prospers as a useless though intriguing oddball.

The Throwing Knife
Steel: Straight carbon (RC 54 to 56).
Length: Blade 3 to 8 inches, 5 to 12 inches overall.
Tip: Spear with swedge.
Spine: Stiff.
Blade bevel: Flat-ground.
Edge bevel: Cannel, unsharpened.
Handle: Steel, wrapped with rawhide or a soft synthetic.
General information: The steel of a throwing knife should be soft and
    bendable; if it doesn't bend, the knife will break. The constant
    cracking impact of hits—and, far more damaging, misses—will even-
    tually snap standard knife steel, usually at the tip.

Throwing knives should be one piece, with the tang forming the handle. Rivets, slabs, guards, and pommels will eventually be beaten and broken from impact. The only workable handles I've seen on throwing knives are vinyl and leather. The steel tang is dipped into the vinyl to form a very thin coating. The leather or a synthetic substitute is simply wrapped rawhide. Neither makes for a particularly comfortable handle, but the cushioning effect does dampen the stinging crack of a miss. Too, a wide, comfortable handle on a throwing knife would interfere with the balance of the airborne blade.

For a knife to be thrown properly, it must have a point in perfect line with the center of the handle and be double-edged, with a fast, wide flair at the tip. Although the tip should be pointed and sharp, the edge should be dull and incapable of cutting. You hold a knife at the tip to throw it—and you're asking for a cut if you sharpen that leading edge. The blade should be longer than the handle, and balance is critical too. A fine throwing knife should balance where the guard would normally occur, at the point where blade joins handle.

Two techniques are employed in throwing a knife. Skillful close-distance throwing (up to 15 feet) depends on correctly judging the number of revolutions a knife will make in the air. Hold the knife at the tip, in such a way that it feels comfortable in your hand, and flip it at the target. Your eyes should be fast enough to determine how it's hitting—handle first or flat-siding. Obviously, if it hits correctly, it will stick.

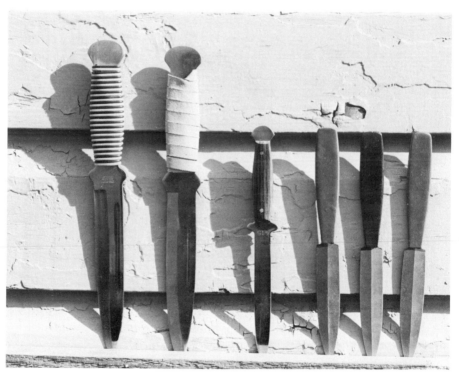

Strength, simplicity, and balance mark a knife as a thrower. Conventional knives, with their multiplicity of parts and hard steel, will not hold together under constant, stinging impact. (Edge, Valor, Pro-throw, Coast Cutlery, Coast Cutlery, Coast Cutlery)

Different lengths, weights, and shapes impart separate characteristics to throwing knives when they are airborne. For regular hits, practice with one knife only, or buy a matched set. (Coast Cutlery Co.)

Adjust the whirl of the knife to your distance from the target by taking a step backward or forward. Once you get the distance down, you'll be able to drive the point home every time.

When you become practiced at this, you'll also discover that you can control the speed of revolutions by the amount of flip you use in your wrist. This is how you stick a knife without pacing off predetermined distances. By knowing the number of flips it will take to make one complete revolution, you can estimate and adjust the number it will take to reach the target. Needless to say, it's important to practice with just one knife or with several knives that are identical.

I'm good up to about 20 feet, or three revolutions of my knife, using this approach. Beyond that, the computations get to be too much for me, and I helicopter the knife. This is done by holding the blade at the tip so the edge rests against the skin between your thumb and index finger. Throw the knife by both flipping it and snapping your hand down so a helicopterlike whirl is imparted to the blade.

This throwing technique makes the knife whirl around the axis of the hilt like a helicopter blade. Since the blade is longer than the handle, the tip of the knife tends to strike objects first, and the weight of the steel behind the point drives it home.

Throwing a knife for short distances is easiest if you hold the tip between your thumb and the large knuckle of your forefinger.

For long-distance throwing, the trick is to make the blade whirl rapidly in the air. Hold the knife at the very tip and snap your hand down as you throw. This makes the blade spin in the air like the blades of a helicopter.

COLLECTOR'S KNIVES

Collecting knives is a hobby all its own that has increased in popularity in the last decade, and it's not surprising. Knives, like jewelry and gold, hold or increase their value as the worth of the original dollar that bought them decreases. There is also the matter of speculation. A custom-made knife bought from a maker just getting into the business could well quadruple in value if that obscure maker becomes famous. Finally, there is that hard-to-define element that makes collecting anything an absorbing pastime. Some people collect minerals, some coins, and others stamps. What better way for a sportsman to satisfy his urge to collect than to gather together examples of one of the basic tools of his trade, the knife?

While knife collections can be nothing more than an array of blades and types that appeal to your fancy, the most attractive collections are based on some sort of theme. The following is a sampling of a few collections I've run across.

• Period collections represent the full spectrum of blades used at some point in history. I've seen one collection based on the cutlery of the 1800s and the bowie knife, with several examples of the bowie design, as well as Arkansas toothpicks, daggers, and other edged weapons and tools of the frontier. Another collection centered on World War II, with fighting knives, bayonets, and ceremonial daggers from the Allied and Axis nations.

• Custom collections catalogue the efforts of hand knife makers. As a rule, collectors follow one of two persuasions: they collect either handmade knives that follow established design patterns, striving for a representation of the best of the craftsmen, or they look for knives that are expressions of art and imagination. Examples of the latter types of knife designs would be radically upswept points, graceful curved handles with deep finger cutouts, and unusual or exotic handle and blade materials.

• Collecting the complete line of knives a manufacturer has produced since the founding of the company is yet another ambitious project.

There are many other possible themes for knife collections: knives for unusual jobs or knives with unusual construction features. A friend once gave me a slicing-and-scraping knife that looked a little like a

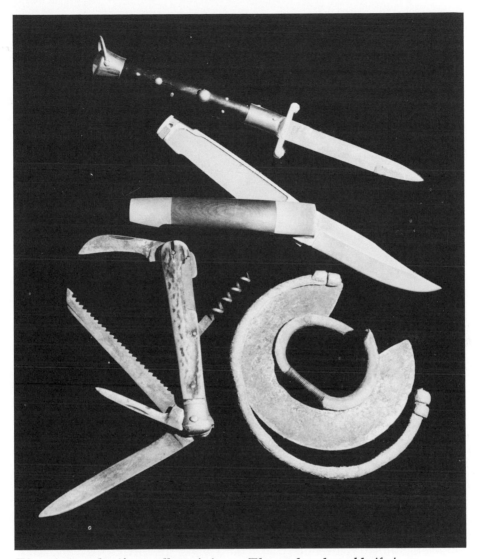

*These knives classify as collector's items. The washer-shaped knife is an
African wrist knife, with its unique sheath partially removed. The folding
knife (second from left) is unusual for its butterfly opening and the fact
that it's made by one of the better-known contemporary custom knife makers,
Barry Woods. The sale and manufacture of switchblades have been
banned in this country, making any switchblade worthy of collection, and the
five-bladed folder is the original Swiss Army knife issued around 1900,
incorporating a locking master blade (unusual in itself on a multibladed folder),
a saw, an awl, a pruning blade, and a corkscrew for opening wine bottles.*

These knives were all handmade, not by professionals but by homesteaders and hunters who perceived a way to fill their cutting needs. The light-handled skinning knife was fashioned from an old automobile coil. The large big-game knife with Bowie lines was made by a Cree Indian for elk and moose hunting. It was originally the pressure plate on a bulldozer. The butcher knife came to this country with German emigrants, and the boner arrived with Polish settlers. Both of these knives are still in use today and are excellent cutting tools. Note the cant on both blades; many modern commercial manufacturers have recently recognized the value of this feature.

large washer. It was from Africa, and it was worn on the wrist, like jewelry. This is surely a collector's knife. The various types of switchblades manufactured in the past would make an interesting collection, as would knives representative of a particular culture. In fact, the type of collection you pursue is limited only by your imagination.

Identifying Knife Value

There are certain features that identify a knife as a valuable collector's item. Hand manufacture is one.

If a knife is truly handmade, it will usually show some imperfections. Knife makers traditionally identify themselves either by their name or by a hallmark stamped in the blade. Famous makers of the past can be traced down through these brands, and so can present-day craftsmen. The best knife makers in this country belong to the Knife-makers Guild, and you can obtain a list by writing a member. Morseth Knives, 1705 Highway 71 N., Springdale, Arkansas 72764, and Bob Dozier, Box 58, Palmetto, Louisiana 71358, are both fine knife makers and members of the guild. (The guild "headquarters" changes annually with the new secretary.)

Engraving and inlay work is another sign of value. Just how much value the art adds to the blade is determined by the quality of inlay, detail, and the materials used. The finest inlays will show no seam. Engravings that incorporate exquisite detail—such as textured hair on big-game animals, feathering on birds, or buttons on a man's shirt—will be worth far more than simple scrollwork. Gold, platinum, or jeweled inlays will be worth more than ivory or silver.

Uniqueness adds value. When a blade or a knife is one of a kind, it becomes worthy of collection. Antiquity is another indicator of worth. For example, a good friend of mine has a one-piece hunting knife fashioned from an old car spring. The handle is the same steel as the blade, and the blade was ground down to a point where it's filet-limber. The profile of the knife looks almost like a scimitar. It was some settler's idea of what a hunting knife should be and do, and, although it hardly matches practical modern guidelines, its age and uniqueness give it value. My friend has been offered $50 for that knife.

Realize, however, that antiquity is a relative thing. You'll run into an awful lot of rusty jackknives that were made within the last twenty years and not cared for. Because of this interest in knife collection, several manufacturers are now dating their blades by symbols. Case Cutlery, for example, stamps a series of dots (referred to by collectors as "measles") into the steel on the flat of the blade near the holster. Eight dots mean 1972, five dots 1975, and so forth. When we hit 1980, they plan to relocate the position of the dots and begin with ten again.

Part III

Food Knives

THE MAJORITY OF FOOD KNIVES are used for slicing; consequently, they don't require the inherent strength of dropped-V grinds or a thick spine. Their blade stiffness usually runs from medium to limber, and their thinness is advantageous for slicing and sharpening.

Food knives are available in a full range of steels and alloys. Stainless alloys are the most popular steels for kitchenware, and carbon steels are the common choice of chefs. The steel for food knives does not have to be so hard as that for outdoor knives because the materials needed to sharpen food knives are always in reach. I've enjoyed excellent performance from straight carbon blades with an RC rating of 56, but such "soft" steel is hard to find. Knife makers seem to be in some sort of hardness competition, and RC's of 58 to 60 are the norm, especially in the stainless steels.

The bevels ground onto these knives include double-edge, hollow ground, concave, scalloped, and serrated. Each edge has its place in cooking, but no one edge will do everything.

Handles on food knives are usually made of Pakkawood, wood, or a synthetic, and they're affixed to full, half, or push tangs. These knives are not normally subject to the physical pressures endured by shop and outdoor knives, but they are assaulted by frequent washings.

Signs of quality on top-notch food knives, aside from their steel, include rivets ground flush with the handle and close tolerances between handle slabs, tangs, and blades. Food knives seldom have guards, since they would get in the way of much of the work. In place of guards, the best food knives have strengthening bolsters.

While food knives are, in general, lighter and more delicate than outdoor or shop knives, they are just as utilitarian. Yet there aren't many cooks who consider their knives as tools, and I think I know the reason why.

Women use kitchen knives, and men use outdoor and shop knives. In the past, there has been a sharp line drawn between the male and female "mystique" and their respective roles. Females were trained in the housewifely arts but not in the manly trades; thus, the idea of the proficient use of tools wasn't a usual concern for women.

My research helps confirm the suspicion. Because there has been so little written about knives, a great deal of my information came by way of personal interviews. Although the women I spoke to all used knives every day, only a few noted any significant differences among the blades in their kitchen, and none of these could give me explicit reasons for the differences they did see.

Information about food knives has always come from professional chefs—males who were quick to grasp the fact that a bread knife is as much a tool of the cooking trade as is a chisel or a plane a tool of carpentry.

These chefs, too, had the most knives. Their experience taught them that different kitchen cutting jobs required slightly different edges and blades. One chef at a well-known Southampton, Long Island, restaurant had twenty-two distinctly different knives. Among them were two narrow slicing knives, one with a stiff spine for boned roasts and one with a limber spine that would bend around the contours of a standing rib roast.

Of course, such a selection is not necessary for private kitchens. But I'm a knife nut, and we have fifteen different types of knives in our kitchen for preparing and serving food, plus another seven for butchering jobs. Although you should let the type and scope of food preparation you enjoy define your selection, there is a starting point. I can't imagine any kitchen without four basic blades: the French chef's knife, a parer, some sort of meat slicer, and a utility knife.

KITCHEN KNIVES

Although every blade discussed in this chapter could well be found in the kitchen, let's define kitchen knives as those you would use in your kitchen to prepare and cook any food but meats and fish.

French Chef's Knife
Steel: Straight carbon, carbon alloy, stainless alloy.
Length: Blade 4 to 12 inches, 8 to 16 inches overall.
Tip: Slender spear in line with the center of the handle.
Spine: Medium.
Blade bevel: V grind. Blade deep in profile with heel.
Edge bevel: 30 to 36 degrees on a rockered double-edge bevel.
Handle: Pakkawood, synthetic wood handle flush with knife back.
General information: The French chef's knife has rightfully been called
the queen of the kitchen. It is an all-purpose vegetable knife with
easily recognizable characteristics: a handle that's in line with the
knife back, a deep-throated blade, and a rockered edge. There's a
reason for each of these features.

The handle in line with the back, coupled with the heeled blade,
affords room for your knuckles. You can slice fully through a potato
or turnip, and you can slice down to the cutting board using any part
of the edge. A handle in line with the edge would not afford this
latitude—you would have to cut with the tip section of the knife, and
even then your knuckles would scrape the board.

A rockered edge is one that is rounded. It appears to be gently
curved, like rockers on a chair. When cutting against a board, the
rockered edge is a more efficient slicer than a straight edge because you
can bring pressure to bear on the exact part of the blade that's doing
the cutting.

To grasp this principle more fully, lay a piece of stationery on a
cutting board and try to slice it with a straight knife edge. It will be
difficult to do, since the entire edge is working at cutting the full sheet
of paper. Now try the same procedure with a rockered edge. Only that
part of the edge touching the board does the cutting. It cuts small sections at a time, yet one full stroke with a rockered edge will easily cut
the paper in half.

The deep-throated blade of this knife protects your knuckles, and
it also promotes uniform slicing. The broad span of steel acts as a guide.
It lies flat against the onion or beet it's slicing and resists twisting or
curving as you cut downward. Once you make the first cut, the blade
follows that pattern straight and true. Uniform slicing will be further

promoted if you select a blade bevel that's a V or straight grind. Hollow or concave grinds tend to throw the blade off to the side. This knife is also a chopper, so a hollow grind, which makes for a weak edge area, would be inefficient for the purpose.

The blade design, the placement of the handle, and the rockered edge on a chef's knife lend themselves to yet another kitchen chore that alone makes it worth having: it enables you to dice and mince with mechanical ease.

To dice with this knife, either hold the tip between thumb and forefinger of your left hand (if you're right-handed) or apply downward pressure on the tip section of the knife back with the flat of your hand. Then grasp the handle (I like to hold it between my thumb and forefinger) and rapidly raise and lower the handle while you hold the tip down. You'll note that the knife rocks on its rounded edge. Slip a slice of onion or a stalk of celery under the rear half of the blade, and, as you chop, swing the blade from the tip in a quarter-circle arc. The vegetable will be diced in a matter of seconds.

For even finer dicing, use the blade as a scraper to gather and mound the diced vegetables—and chop some more. If you repeat the process several times, you'll end up with a mince.

A chef once showed me an interesting variation on this dicing technique: using his index fingers as spacers, and his thumb and middle fingers to pinch the blades and handles, he dices with two chef's knives at once. Coleslaw literally flies in his kitchen!

When selecting a chef's knife, be sure the blade length is appropriate for the job you're expecting the knife to do. Large vegetables like turnips, Bermuda onions, cabbages, and whole celery require a 10- or 12-inch blade for a uniform, one-stroke cut and efficient dicing. Beets, carrots, and celery can be sliced and diced with a 6-to-8-inch blade. If your tastes include a lot of minced garlic and onion, you'll probably find the lightness and speed of a 4-to-5-inch blade an immeasurable help. It's been my experience that a serious cook finds a use for all three lengths in the course of preparing a meal.

left: *The French chef's knife is the most
useful design of all kitchenware.
(Gustav Ern, Cutco, Interpur)*

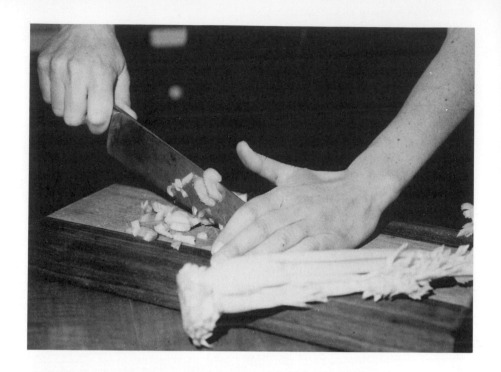

top left: *To dice with the French chef's knife, hold the tip down with one hand and rapidly raise and lower the handle with the other. At the same time, swing the blade in an arc with the knife tip acting as the pivot point.*

bottom left: *The broad blade may be used as a scraper to pile the cut vegetables and prepare for even finer dicing.*

top right: *When you become adept at using this knife, finely diced celery takes only a few seconds to prepare. Continue chopping and you'll end up with a mince.*

Paring Knife
Steel: Stainless alloy, carbon alloy.
Length: Blade 3 to 4 inches, 7 to 8 inches overall.
Tip: Spear or clip.
Spine: Medium.
Blade bevel: Straight, hollow, or concave grind.
Edge bevel: 24 to 30 degrees, double edge.
Handle: Pakkawood, synthetic, wood.

General information: Paring knives are for delicate handwork like root-
ing a spot of rot out of a potato, trimming the end off a carrot, or
peeling an onion. (These are also the knives to use for peeling
things like potatoes and apples if you use a knife for these tasks;
I think slotted peelers are faster and safer.)

Fine blade and point work dictates a short blade of around 4
inches. Remember that a comfortable fit in your hand is essential to

*Paring and peeling are exacting work, and a short blade allows delicate
control. Cutting with the tip will be easiest if the point falls close to the
centerline of the handle. (Gustav Ern)*

blade control, and small knives tend to have too-small handles. The blade should be slender when viewed from the edge or back, and it should not be deep in profile. A paring knife must be capable of round cuts and curlicues, so back and edge should fall in close line with the top and bottom of the handle. The most common mistake people make when picking out a paring knife is choosing one with a raised tip. The control required for fine tip paring dictates a dropped point nearly in line with the center of the handle.

Tomato Knives

Steel: Stainless alloy or stainless.
Length: Blade 6 to 8 inches, 10 to 12 inches overall.
Tip: Scimitar, needle, or rigging. Slender and sharp pointed.
Spine: Limber, medium limber.
Blade bevel: Straight, concave, or hollow ground.
Edge bevel: Scalloped or serrated edge, 24 to 30 degrees.
Handle: Pakkawood, synthetic, wood.
General information: Tomato knives are in a class by themselves because the acids in these fruits dull a carbon steel edge and because ripe tomatoes will not tolerate any pressure as you slice. Stainless blades resist the dulling effects of the acid best, and a scalloped or serrated edge creates the sawing effect you'll need to slice cleanly through the soft, pulpy flesh.

Tomato knives should have at least a 6-inch blade. As with any slicing knife, you'll get a more uniform and attractive result if you can cut the slab in one stroke. Remember, though, that tomatoes buckle under pressure.

The importance of "making a fast, firm cut" is one myth about slicing tomatoes that I can personally lay to rest. Several years ago a good friend of mine bought one of those do-it-all vegetable slicers for his wife. One of the jobs this gadget was reputed to do was slice perfect rounds of tomato. As the TV ad went, you just put the fruit between the top and bottom of the press, pushed firmly, and the slices came tumbling out, cleaved as cleanly as a roll of shiny new coins.

The women were shopping that afternoon, and neither my friend nor I could contain our curiosity. He picked the reddest, ripest tomato in his garden, nestled it in the press, and began a brief debate.

"Should we push gently? Or should we be firm and fast?"

Firm and fast won because of technical considerations like fluid resistance and the relative resiliency of a tomato. My friend's background played a part too: he holds a black belt in judo and is therefore a past master at being firm and fast.

"Are you ready?" he asked, assuming the traditional stance.

I nodded, and he let fly with a magnificent hand chop that shook the timbers under the kitchen floor.

When the tomato storm subsided, there were juice, pulp, seeds, and tiny bits of red skin everywhere, which still weren't mopped up and washed off when our wives got back two hours later. As a matter of fact, we are still finding stray seeds—and belly-laughing all over again —four years later.

So "firm and fast" is not the way, though you'll make cleaner cuts

The acids in tomatoes and citrus fruit dull carbon steel, so stainless is preferred for these knives. Since the pulpy interior of these fruits is more easily torn apart than cut, a scalloped or serrated edge is a wise choice. (Case, Case)

and find easier slicing if you first puncture the skin at the place where your cut is to begin. You'll need a sharp, slender point to do this.

Citrus Knives
Steel: Stainless alloy, stainless.
Length: Blade 4 to 5 inches, 8 to 9 inches overall.
Tip: Spear.
Spine: Limber and curved near the tip.
Blade bevel: Flat ground. Blade sharpened on both sides.
Edge bevel: 30 to 36 degrees, scalloped or serrated.
Handle: Pakkawood, synthetic, wood.
General information: Citrus fruits dull steel as easily as do tomatoes, and for essentially the same reason. Tomato knives should be used to slice an orange or grapefruit in half, or into quarter sections, but special citrus knives are better for slicing the fruit from the skin when you want a fully sectioned half grapefruit for breakfast.
The blade on these knives curves away from the spine line near the tip, thereby conforming to the fruit's interior. The soft insides of an

The curved blade of a citrus knife cuts fruit free of the skin from the inside. The double edge allows you to cut in two directions. (NA, NA, Geneva Forge)

orange are every bit as unforgiving as a tomato, so cutting citrus meat requires a sawlike edge. The knife is also sharpened on both sides so you can work in either direction.

Bread Knives
Steel: Stainless.
Length: 10 to 12 inches, 14 to 16 inches overall.
Tip: Coping, sheep foot, rounded.
Spine: Medium.
Blade bevel: Flat, hollow or concave ground.
Edge bevel: Serrated or scalloped.
Handle: Pakkawood, synthetic, wood.

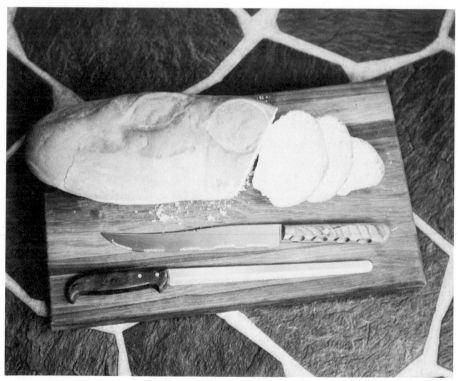

Bread knives don't cut in the classic sense; they tease airy dough apart. A close-patterned scalloped edge or serrated edge does this job best. (Case, Imperial)

General information: Bread knives don't cut in the conventional sense; rather they rip, tear, and tease the soft bread apart. At this job, the serrated edge excels.

The bread knife needs nothing more than a blunted point. You'll cut the most uniform slices if you can lop them off with one stroke, so a 10-to-12-inch blade is best.

When you're cutting bread—especially fresh, warm bread—any sort of downward pressure on the blade will compress the center of the loaf into a doughy mass before the edge will cut, and the slice is not likely to recover. To keep this from happening, don't exert any more pressure than the weight of the blade, even if you have to do some sawing. When you reach the tough bottom crust, you can bring heavy pressure to bear on the tip.

Cake and Pastry Knives

Steel: Stainless.
Length: Blade 5 to 6 inches, 9 inches overall.
Tip: A blunted wedge.
Spine: Medium.
Blade bevel: Flat ground. Blade triangular.
Edge bevel: Rounded edge.
Handle: Pakkawood, metal, synthetic.
General information: Pastry knives function as both a knife to cut and a spatula to lift the cake or pie onto the plate.

Cutting cake can be a constant source of frustration, particularly when the cake is fresh and moist and covered with gooey icing. The problem is basically this: you can't slice most cakes, so you have to cut straight down, which tends to compress the cake. Icing also clings to the flat of the blade, which makes the cutting surface about as smooth as a steel pot scrubber. If the cake doesn't compress, it crumbles as the gooey blade moves down.

The traditional broad-bladed cake knife is probably the worst design for cutting pastry because there's so much blade for the icing to cling to. It's a great gadget for lifting cake or pie onto a plate, but for the actual cutting the best tool I've found is the skinniest, thinnest, sharpest blade in the house; a filet knife. If, however, you insist on being a traditionalist, try either wetting or heating the blade of a cake knife before you cut.

Soft Cheese Knife
Steel: Stainless.
Length: Blade 2 to 3 inches, 4 to 5 inches overall.
Tip: Broad and rounded.
Spine: Limber.
Blade bevel: Flat ground, blade deep in profile.
Edge bevel: None.
Handle: Pakkawood, synthetic, wood, steel, silver.
General information: The soft cheese knife is used for spreading, so it
    is limber and unsharpened and has a palettelike tip. A highly
    polished finish is advantageous, since the glassy surface allows the
    cheese to slip and slide off the blade and onto a cracker or piece of
    bread. With a satin-finish blade, the cheese tends to stick to the
    knife. Cheese knives are usually serving knives, so their handles are
    often decorative. Typical cheeses that are spread instead of sliced
    are boursin, Liederkranz, cream, Roquefort, and soft cheddar
    cheeses.

Hard Cheese Knife
Steel: Stainless.
Length: Blade 4 to 6 inches, 8 to 10 inches overall.
Tip: Rounded, coping, sheep foot.
Spine: Medium, medium-stiff.
Blade bevel: Flat ground.
Edge bevel: Single edge or scalloped, 36 to 48 degrees.
Handle: Pakkawood, synthetic, wood, steel, silver.
General information: Block cheeses—for example, American, Swiss,
    and provolone—require a special knife. This type of cheese has a
    clinging, sticky quality as you cut it, so when you use a knife with
    a double bevel the thin slice of cheese sticks to the blade and the
    slice crumbles before the cut is finished.
        To counter this tendency, hard-cheese knives work best if they
have a single-edge bevel on a 36-to-48-degree angle. The flat side of the
knife faces the block, and the beveled side faces the slice. As the blade
is forced downward, the edge cuts and the bevel peels the slice away
from the face of the blade.
        Cheese knives need not be much longer than the width of the
block you're cutting because the slice is made by forcing the blade

Knives for soft cheeses, like bleu and Camembert, are spreading knives.
They should be flexible, broad, and highly polished. Hard
cheeses, like Swiss and block cheddar, are prone to stick and bind to a knife
blade; hence, a highly polished knife with a single-edge bevel works best.
(Clockwise: Super Edge, Regent, Westmark, Case, NA)

down with minimal stroking motion. You'll get the most even slices with a deep-profile blade, since the large edge area will function like a guide as it slides down the face of the block of cheese. A quality flat-ground blade with a scalloped edge is acceptable—it is essentially a single-edge bevel.

Slicing cheese perfectly is a challenge that has taxed many an imagination. Two of the more workable variations on the cheese knife that I've run across include a thin piece of piano wire stretched between two steel arms. The wire cuts cheese without any binding, but it's difficult to make uniform slices with this instrument.

Another interesting blade is a rather standard-looking cheese knife with a hollow ground into each side of the blade. It breaks the cheese-to-steel friction and cuts uniform slices without crumbling the cheese.

MEAT KNIVES

Meat cutting can be divided into three stages: butchering, preparing the meat for cooking, and carving for the table. Most meat knives should have a sharper edge than kitchen knives do. You'll find a 24- to 30-degree bevel most satisfactory. I prefer carbon steel, though there is an inherent contradiction in that preference. Meat cutting—especially carving hot meat—dulls carbon steel by certain chemical processes which take place. This would logically point to stainless steel.

With due respect to logic, I've found that practice hasn't supported theory. Although I've certainly tried them enough, I discovered that the stainless steels are not the meat cutters that straight carbons are. The same may be said for scalloped edges; a straight edge regularly turns out the most perfect slices for me.

Boning Knives
Steel: Straight carbon, carbon alloy, stainless alloy.
Length: Blade 4 to 8 inches, 8 to 12 inches overall.
Tip: Needle or slender scimitar.
Spine: Medium, medium limber.
Blade bevel: V grind. Blade very slim in profile, sometimes canted
      upward.
Edge bevel: 24 to 30 degrees.
Handle: Pakkawood, synthetic, wood.
General information: The boning knife is used to separate meat from
      bone. It is a brother to the filet knife in design and function,
      though the boning knife has a stiffer spine.
      Boning knives have a thin blade profile—¾ inch to 1 inch deep at
the hilt—tapering up to a fine, sharp point that's either in line with the
back of the knife or canted upward. This design allows deep, probing
cuts that can be curved to conform to bone contours. A boning knife
that has a canted blade is advantageous when you're fileting meat from
a flat surface like a shoulder blade, but it makes removal of meat from
round bones and joints a bit more difficult than a knife with a straight
blade.

If you're planning on butchering large animals—beef or big game—
you'll need two boning knives, one with a 7- to 8-inch blade for deep
cuts around shoulder blades and hams, and another with a 4-inch blade
for fine work around joints and loins. The 4-inch boning knife also has

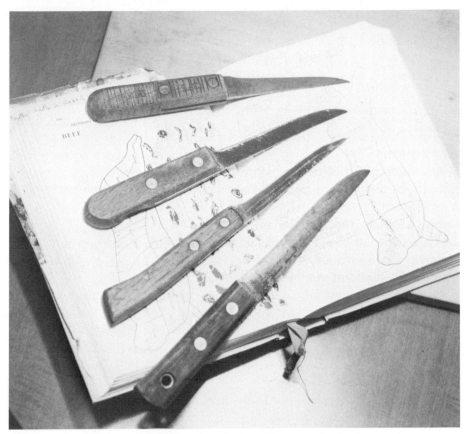

Large boning knives are used for butchering. Four- to five-inch boning knives are useful in the kitchen and for fine cutting work around joints. (Goodell, Flint, J. K. Adams, Dexter)

many uses in the preparation of food. Breasting out fowl and trimming up the leftovers of a rib roast for croquettes or sandwiches are examples of the kitchen work this knife is designed for.

Boning knives honed to shaving sharpness filet meat most efficiently, but the inevitable contact with bone dulls the fine edge quickly. Some prying with the edge may also be required, and this will nick such an acute bevel. For general boning work, then, use an edge of around 24 to 30 degrees.

The boning process is a little like skinning. After an initial incision down to the bone, one hand peels the meat free while the other cuts. Since 95 percent of the cutting work will be within an inch of the tip, keep checking this area for sharpness. Another thing to remember is that close-cutting meat from bone is a wrist action rather than a stroke of the arm. A person adept with a boning knife can separate pounds of flesh with one quick, accurate sweep of his wrist, but a beginner is better off taking small, mincing strokes; otherwise, he risks leaving a lot of meat that will be good only for hamburger.

Butcher Knife
Steel: Straight carbon, carbon alloy, stainless alloy.
Length: Blade 10 to 14 inches, 14 to 18 inches overall.
Tip: Clip.
Spine: Medium, medium limber.
Blade bevel: Flat or V grind. Blade deep in profile.
Edge bevel: 18 to 24 degrees, double edge.
Handle: Pakkawood, synthetic, wood.
General information: Butcher knives are used to slice steaks and chops
     and to cut roasts from whole carcasses. The blade on a butcher
     knife should be long—I prefer one 12 to 14 inches—and it should
     be 2 to 3 inches deep. This depth helps guide the knife to more
     uniform cuts. A slight heel on the blade prevents knuckle-dusting
     against the cutting board.

     The trick to cutting uniform steaks and chops is to keep your slicing to a minimum. If you can lop a steak off with one stroke, so much the better. Begin your cut close to the handle and draw the knife to you, shifting pressure from the handle to the tip as it slices through the meat. A rocking motion in which your cutting stroke describes an arc makes the most efficient use of the edge. If the steak is too large to be sliced with one stroke, repeat the process.

     Don't saw through meat with a butcher knife; make all your cuts in the same direction or you'll end up with an uneven slice of meat. Cut through a hard bone with a bone saw and a soft bone with a cleaver. Then continue the slice with the butcher knife. Don't let the edge of the knife come in hard contact with the bone, as this quickly dulls the best knife steel.

Utility Knife
Steel: Stainless alloy, carbon alloy, straight carbon.
Length: Blade 6 to 8 inches, 10 to 12 inches overall.
Tip: Clip, rigging.
Spine: Medium limber, medium.

The utility knife is the most popular kitchen cutlery of all. It is useful both as a meat and vegetable knife, though it is not so able as those knives designed for specific cutting jobs. (Cutco, Royal)

Blade bevel: Flat; occasionally hollow or concave grind.
Edge bevel: 30 degrees, double edge.
Handle: Pakkawood, synthetic, wood.
General information: The utility knife is a kind of catchall design that looks like a small version of the butcher knife. It is a capable blade as a vegetable knife and a meat knife, but it is not really the perfect knife for any one type of cutting job. Still, its all-around nature has persistent appeal, and this knife ranks as the most popular kitchen cutlery piece of all. You'll find it a part of virtually every food knife collection—yet, once you become familiar with specific knives and their function, the utility knife usually will become the least-used blade in the rack.

Steak Scimitar
Steel: Straight carbon, carbon alloy, stainless alloy.
Length: Blade 12 to 14 inches, 16 to 18 inches overall.
Tip: Scimitar.
Spine: Medium, medium limber.

A fine quartet of professional butchering and carving knives: a butcher knife, a cleaver, a roast beef slicer, and a steak scimitar. (Case, Case, Ontario Knife Co., Ontario Knife Co.)

Blade bevel: Flat or V grind, rockered edge.
Edge bevel: 18 to 24 degrees.
Handle: Pakkawood, synthetic, wood.
General information: The steak scimitar is used to slab whole steaks from a large carcass. It is better at this particular job than a butcher knife, though not so useful for cutting chops and roasts. When slicing steaks, use the scimitar the same way as you would a butcher knife.

Narrow Slicer or Ham Slicer
Steel: Straight carbon, carbon alloy, stainless alloy.
Length: Blade 10 to 12 inches, 12 to 16 inches overall.
Tip: Sheep foot, coping, slender rigging.
Spine: Limber, medium limber.
Blade bevel: Flat or V grind; occasionally hollow or concave ground. Blade very narrow in profile.
Edge bevel: Single and double bevel, 18 to 24 degrees.
Handle: Pakkawood, synthetic, wood. On decorative slicers, steel or silver.

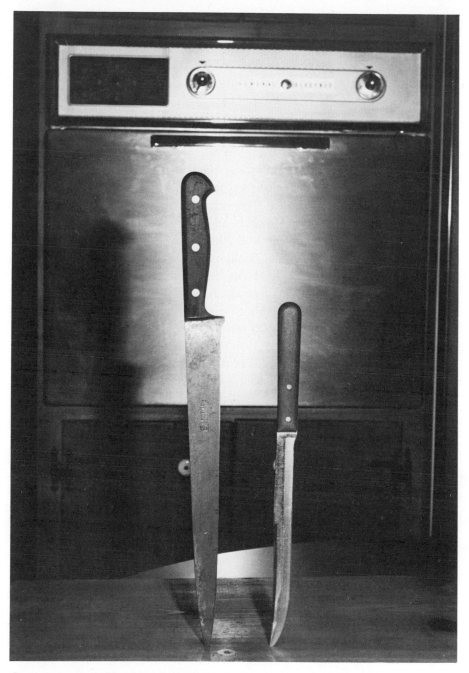

Carving knives differ from butchering knives in that they slice hot meat. These are two typical kitchen meat knives: a carving knife and a narrow slicer. (Gustav Ern, Craftsman)

General information: The narrow slicer, or ham slicer, is used to slice
   portions of meat from cooked roasts. Its narrow profile facilitates
   contour slicing, as opposed to the straight slicing job the butcher
   knife does.

Chefs prefer this blade over the carving knife for most hot-meat
slicing. They choose a carving knife only when they have to work around
a lot of bone. For example, they use the narrow slicer to slab off the
prime meat from a turkey breast or ham roast; they use the carving
knife to clean up what is left close to the bone.

A narrow slicer—any knife that is primarily a slicer, for that matter
—will perform best if it has a thin blade. A wide-spined, medium-to-
stiff blade requires a steep-pitched blade bevel, which in turn makes
thin, even slicing very difficult. A slicing knife with a wide blade bevel
tends to wobble or waver as you cut down, since the side of the blade
has a natural tendency to lie flat against the meat being cut. This in
turn forces the center of the spine out of alignment with the edge, so
as you cut downward, the blade fails to track correctly, producing an
uneven slice.

An interesting solution to this problem is a knife with a straight
blade bevel and a single-bevel edge. The flat blade hugs the meat as you
slice, and if you hold the knife so the edge bevel angles away from the
roast and into the slice, the spine and cutting edge will always be in
perfect alignment. I've also been told by several chefs that a single-
bevel edge will retain its keenness longer than will a double-bevel edge
when you're cutting hot meat, though I cannot ascertain why.

Wide Slicer or Roast Beef Slicer
Steel: Straight carbon, carbon alloy.
Length: Blade 12 to 14 inches, 16 to 18 inches overall.
Tip: Rounded.
Spine: Limber, medium limber.
Blade bevel: Flat. Blade 2 to 3 inches deep in profile.
Edge bevel: 18 to 24 degrees, single or double bevel.
Handle: Pakkawood, synthetic, wood.
General information: The roast beef slicer is excellent as a slicer for
   any hot boned meat. It is not a very able knife for contour cutting.

Carving Knife
Steel: Straight carbon, carbon alloy, stainless alloy.
Length: Blade 9 to 12 inches, 12 to 16 inches overall.

Tip: Slender spear.

Spine: Medium, medium limber.

Blade bevel: V or flat grind, sometimes hollow or concave grind. Blade has shallow heel.

Edge bevel: Double edge, 18 to 24 degrees.

Handle: Pakkawood, synthetic, wood; horn, silver on decorative carvers.

General information: Carving knives can be subject to some interesting though improper interpretations because of their ornamental nature. I once received a carving set imported from India, for example, and the blade on the knife strongly resembled a bowie knife.

A carving knife, whether ornamental or not, should possess the qualities of a meat slicer: a long blade for uniform slices and a medium-to-limber blade stiffness. It should have a slender tip for contour cut-

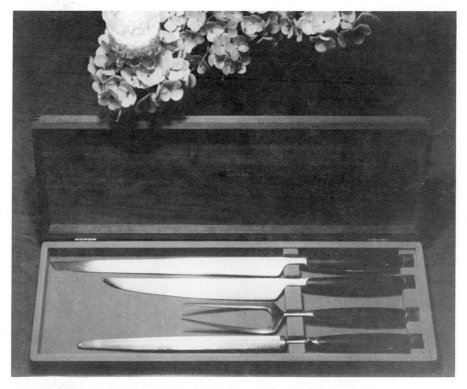

This ornamental but functional carving set contains a narrow slicer, a carving knife, a serving fork, and a sharpening steel. (Lauffer)

ting. To some extent, these knives represent a marriage of other meat cutters; in the course of table-carving duties they're called upon to bone, slice, and cut. You'll find, however, that they are not substitutes for these other knives; a boning knife bones more efficiently, a butcher knife cuts more uniform steaks; and a narrow slicer is more capable of producing paper-thin slabs of ham or turkey.

Cold-Cut Knife
Steel: Stainless, stainless alloy.
Length: Blade 7 to 9 inches, 11 to 13 inches overall.
Tip: Rigging or scimitar.
Spine: Medium limber.
Blade bevel: Flat ground, concave or hollow ground. Shallow heel
　　　on blade.

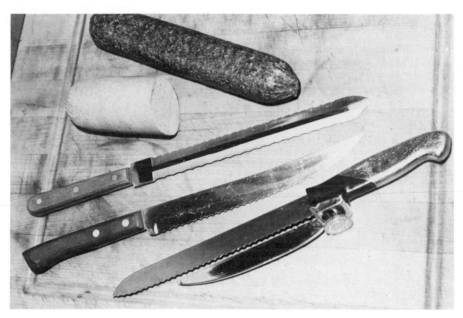

Many cold cuts will bind a conventional edge, so a hollow-ground scalloped edge is preferred. A sharp point is occasionally needed to pierce tough casings. The top knife has two interesting design variations: a double edge of coarse and fine scallops and a forked tip to pick up sliced meat. The knife at the bottom has an adjustable guide that gauges the thickness of each slice and helps keep it uniform. (Centurion, Flint, Magna)

Edge bevel: 24 to 30 degrees, scalloped.

Handle: Pakkawood, synthetic, wood.

General information: Cold cuts are a little like hard cheese in that they tend to bind the blade. A scalloped edge partially negates this tendency. The best cold-cut knives will have a flat blade bevel and a hollow grind. This blade-and-edge relationship overcomes binding even more than the scalloped edge alone. The sharp point is occasionally needed to puncture the tough skin of cold cuts before making a slice. Some cold-cut knives have double points, so the knife may be used as a fork to pick up the slabs of meat.

Frozen Food Knife

Steel: Stainless, stainless alloy.

Length: Blade 6 to 8 inches, 10 to 12 inches overall.

Tip: Coping, sheep foot, forked.

Spine: Medium, medium stiff.

Blade bevel: Flat ground.

Frozen food knives save many foods that would otherwise be wasted; they will cut a package of meat in two so you can avoid the tedium of hamburgers two days in a row. (Ekco)

Edge bevel: Scalloped, serrated, or some variation of sawtooth.

Handle: Pakkawood, synthetic, wood.

General information: The frozen meat knife is a type of saw that cuts through frozen foods, so the edges on these knives are often in a class by themselves. They're useful tools: when you have hamburger for four, and two people eating, with this knife you don't have to find a use for the other half of the package; just cut it in half and return it to the freezer.

Most serrated or scalloped edges will work as freezer knives. Don't, however, use a knife with a concave- or hollow-ground edge. It isn't strong enough to take the substantial pressure needed to saw through hard-frozen foods.

Meat Cleaver

Steel: Straight carbon, carbon alloy.

Length: Blade 4 to 8 inches, 8 to 12 inches overall. Weight, 2 to 4 pounds.

Tip: Square.

Spine: Stiff and massive.

Blade bevel: Flat ground, rolled as it nears the edge.

Edge bevel: Cannel, 36 to 42 degrees.

Handle: High-impact synthetic, wood, Pakkawood.

General information: Cleavers are used to cut cartilage and soft bone: brisket, ribs, and chops on pork and lamb. Cleavers for these large cuts should be large themselves: 4 to 5 pounds in weight with 8 to 10 inches of cutting edge. Because of constant impact against hardwood blocks, cleavers eventually split wooden handles, so a high-impact synthetic is better—so long as it is checkered or otherwise roughened for a firm, slip-free grip.

To cleave meat, the edge must slam down flat against the chopping block. This requires a downward snap of the wrist near the end of the swing. If you fail to cut the meat cleanly, don't try a second swing; you'll never hit in exactly the same spot twice. Instead, leave the edge where it is and hit the back of the cleaver with a leather or wooden mallet (a hammer may break shards of steel off the back). You'll get as clean a cut as if the stroke had been complete.

Smaller cleavers in the 1- to 2-pound category are useful in the kitchen. Use them to section poultry for soups or frying and to cleave seafood.

SEAFOOD KNIVES

Many meat knives may be used on seafood. A butcher knife butchers large fish just as efficiently as it slices steaks from beef, and a light cleaver is the easiest way to cut through thick fishbone. The French chef's knife is another example of a blade that does double duty: it is the perfect tool for splitting a broiled lobster, mincing clams, or dicing shrimp. There are, however, several knives suited specifically to preparing fish and shellfish for the table. As a rule, the blades on these knives should be stainless steel or a stainless alloy. Straight carbon steel and salt water is a combination that's bound to produce rust eventually.

Filet Knives
Steel: Stainless alloy.
Length: Blade 7 to 9 inches, 11 to 13 inches overall.
Tip: Gently curving scimitar, very long and slender.
Spine: Limber. When flexed against a cutting board, it's important that the spine of a filet knife describe a parabolic arc.
Blade bevel: V or flat grind. The blade is extremely slender in profile and is occasionally canted up from the handle.
Edge bevel: Double edge, 18 to 24 degrees.
Handle: Synthetic, Pakkawood, wood.
General information: Filet knives should be light, slim, and limber. They are quite delicate and should be used only for filcting. Cleaning fish (see "Fishing Knives," pages 82–88) and cutting bone are jobs better left to other blades.

Of all common food knives, the filet knife should be the sharpest. A razor edge filets more efficiently, and since such a fine edge will not hold up under heavy cutting, a filet knife should cut only fish flesh.

The most common mistake in fileting fish is to use the tip end of the knife exclusively. Indeed, the tip work is important, but, if you are using a filet knife correctly, the entire edge is brought into play.

The initial incisions are made on either side of the backbone with the front third of the knife edge. Once the flesh is opened, separate meat from bone with a circular sweep of the blade, using your wrist and arm. As you cut, the blade should be at a 30- to 48-degree angle to the backbone, and it should be buried to the bolster.

Draw the knife from head to tail, bringing light pressure to bear on the flat of the blade. The limber blade will hug close to the bones

Filet knives must be razor sharp and should never be used either for cutting fishbone or for scaling a fish. A limber blade conforms best to skeletal contours. (Normark, G&C, Normark, Ludwig Schiff, Ludwig Schiff, Ludwig Schiff)

and leave so little meat that you'll be able to read a newspaper through the flesh that's left. If your technique is correct, you should be able to filet a bone-free slab of meat in two strokes.

Another trick I've learned is to use a filet knife to skin the fish. It's much faster and much less work than scaling it. To do this, leave the fileted meat attached to the tail of the carcass by a thin strip of flesh. The carcass affords a good grip during the skinning process; if you cut the meat free you'll immediately discover that fish skin doesn't have any handles.

Fileting the skin free of the meat is more like shaving than cutting. You pin the skin against the cutting board by putting a lot of downward pressure on the blade. The blade is nearly flat against the board too; the knife back is raised only 12 to 18 degrees. Pull the skin past the knife, as if you were tugging laundry through an old wringer washer, and it will slice free paper-thin. There is no need to cut. In fact, if you try to slice, you'll likely cut through the skin—and will waste five minutes and half your filet trying to establish another handle.

Scaling Knives
Steel: Stainless.
Length: Blade 3 to 4 inches, 7 to 8 inches overall.
Tip: Rounded, coping, sheep foot.

Spine: Stiff.
Blade bevel: Flat ground.
Edge bevel: Serrated or sawteeth, 30 to 36 degrees.
Handle: Synthetic.
General information: You can remove scales from a fish using any
    conventional edge by working against the grain, the grain being the
    direction in which the scales are laid down. A straight edge will
    scale in this manner, but scalloped and serrated edges make even
    better scalers since their sharpened points tend to hook into the
    scales and tug them free.

However, working against the grain results in a snowstorm of fish
scales. They fly everywhere, so do this outside, not in the kitchen.

An easier and cleaner way to scale fish is with blades specifically
designed for this purpose. Fish scalers look more like saws than knives.
They depend on hooking into the fish for their effectiveness: their teeth
dig into scale material and tug the scales free. When the teeth are
sharp and numerous enough, you can work with the grain and eliminate
95 percent of the blizzard.

The most common scaling devices are nothing more than large
serrations ground into the back of a fishing knife. They look a little
like large sawteeth. The most efficient fish scaler I have yet to en-
counter was a 10-inch band of steel bent into a 4-inch oval and affixed to a handle. Serrations graced both edges: one side had large teeth
for big fish; the other side had small teeth. No matter which way you
moved the tool, two rows of serrations went to work, quickly removing
the scales.

Clam Knives
Steel: Stainless alloy.
Length: Blade 3 to 4 inches, 7 to 8 inches overall.
Tip: Rounded.
Spine: Medium.
Blade bevel: Flat ground or very slender V grind.
Edge bevel: Cannel or double edge, 48 to 54 degrees.
Handle: Synthetic, wood.
General information: The clam knife acts as both a wedge and a slicer.
    The edge of the blade is forced between the clam's two shells.
    The tip of the knife then slices the muscles from the shell, and the
    two halves of the shells lie open.

A. Clam knives should have a rounded point and be sharpened no more than 48 degrees. Both features provide protection for the user. The blade should have a thin spine, however, so it slides easily between the shells. (Dexter)

B. Clams are forced open by leverage. Rest the blade lightly against the widest shell opening and curl your fingers around the spine of the knife.

C. Be firm and fast; squeeze with your fingers, at the same time forcing the handle toward the shell.

D. Once you cut the first muscle, you can scrape the rest of the meat free of the shell with the rounded tip of the knife.

Clams are easiest to open from the side, where the crack is the widest between the shells. The job will also be easier if you let the clams lie undisturbed for half an hour before trying to open them. Then handle them carefully; the more they're jiggled around, the tighter they contract their muscles.

Cradle the clam in the palm of your left hand (if you're right-handed) so the widest crack in the shell faces your fingers. Lay the middle of the blade edge against the crack. Curl your fingers around the top of the blade, and use their power and the strength of your right hand to pry the blade into the clam. Be firm and fast, and the blade will slide easily into the clam.

Once you're inside, continue to use leverage until you cut the main muscle. You can then wedge the rest of the clam open. Use the tip of the clam knife to scrape the insides free from their attachments to the shell.

Because of the necessity of doing finger work in close proximity to the blade, and because you're cutting into the palm of your hand, never sharpen a clam knife more acutely than 48 degrees. You're asking for a bad cut, and a sharper edge won't hold up against the hard shell anyway.

Oyster Knives
Steel: Stainless alloy.
Length: Blade 3 to 4 inches, 7 to 8 inches overall.

An oyster knife with an inch-long blade pops open the hinge without the attendant danger of a puncture wound in your palm.

Considerable pressure is required to force entry
into the hinge; but once you're inside, a twist of the
knife blade breaks the hinge with a chewy "pop."

After the hinge has been broken, the large muscle
can be scraped free of the shell with a clam knife.

Tip: Rounded in profile and along the edge.

Spine: Stiff, running down the center of the blade.

Blade bevel: A double-edge blade bevel that is oval on one side of the blade and flat on the other. Some oyster knives are full ovals when viewed as a cross-section of blade.

Edge bevel: None, or from 48 to 54 degrees. Single-edge on half oval, cannel edge on full oval blade.

Handle: Wood, synthetic. This knife is used to stab as much as to slice, so the butt of the handle should fit comfortably in your palm.

General information: Oysters are opened by forcing the tip of this knife into the large opening near the hinge. Once the hinge is broken, the oyster's muscle is cut by scraping the blade tip against the inside of the shell.

Allow the oysters to relax before you try to open them; cool them, undisturbed, for an hour in the refrigerator. Insert the tip of the oyster knife with sure force. Once the tip penetrates, you might have to turn the knife sideways to fully break the hinge. It opens with a chewy kind of "pop."

While I've seen others do it often, I've never been able to open oysters with the same speed and conviction I bring to bear on clams. I can't seem to sneak up on them fast enough, and I'm continually nervous about burying the point of the oyster knife in my palm. This is a common and serious injury.

A safer though slower way to open oysters is with the Weden Oyster Wonder, the invention of a friend of mine whose unique hobby is selling insurance (he's a professional fisherman most of the time). Dick's knife is really nothing more than a standard oyster knife with 1 inch of blade instead of the standard 3 or 4 inches. With this short blade, you can really put pressure on an oyster without worrying about a puncture wound. Once you have broken the hinge, use a clam knife to slice the muscle from the shell.

Scallop Knives

Steel: Stainless, stainless alloy.

Length: Blade 1 to 2 inches, 4½ to 6 inches overall.

Tip: Rounded.

Spine: Limber, medium limber.

Blade bevel: Flat.

Edge bevel: None or 42 to 48 degrees, double edge.

Handle: Synthetic, wood.

General information: Unlike clams and oysters, scallops usually open
by themselves, so this knife isn't often needed to force the shells
apart. The major function of this blade is to scrape the interior
muscle from the two shell halves and to separate the muscle from
the rest of the fleshy inside. This large, round muscle is the edible
part of these shellfish.

*A scallop knife is primarily a scraping tool used to separate
the large scallop muscle from the shell. (Sani-Safe)*

TABLE KNIVES

Table knives are the most frequently used class of cutlery in the
house—and they're also the poorest cutting tools. There's a reason for
their characteristic dullness, however. China is very hard material, and

a sharp knife quickly dulls when it works against a plate. If these knives were so hard that they held an edge after much cutting onto plates, you would ruin your china. The edge would eventually cut through the glaze and scar the glassy finish, which in turn would allow food stains to penetrate and be absorbed by the porous interior.

Less expensive dinnerware like Melmac is softer than china. It scars quite easily, yet it is still hard enough to eventually dull a sharp edge in the process.

There's no real solution to the problem. You have to choose between the cutting ability of a sharp edge and scratched dinnerware, or smooth plates and a knife and fork combination that tends to tear meat rather than cut it. There is, however, a middle ground. A serrated tip makes for a reasonably efficient tool, and so long as it is ground into an unsharpened bevel it won't scar plates.

The Table or Butter Knife
Steel: Stainless, stainless alloy, silver plate, silver.
Length: Blade 4 to 5 inches, 8 to 9 inches overall.
Tip: Rounded.
Spine: Medium limber.
Blade bevel: Flat.
Edge bevel: None on straight edge, fine serrations along the rounded
    tip section.
Handle: Stainless steel, Pakkawood, synthetic, silver.
General information: The butter knife is used as a spreading knife as
    well as a cutting knife—hence the rounded tip. Butter knives—and
    tableware in general—are as much an ornament as they are a tool;
    consequently, the finest settings are made of silver.

There's a comfortable feel to silver eating utensils that other materials can't match, and a creamy gray brilliance that dresses up the simplest meal. While I'm sold on silver for eating, it's also true that silverware tarnishes and requires polishing. The frequency of polishing required depends on the amount of and kinds of pollutants in the air. Sulfides, a byproduct of combustion, tarnish silver rapidly. The large number of autos and home furnaces in large cities makes polishing a weekly job in this kind of environment and, to my way of thinking, limits the use of silverware to special occasions. I refuse to be a slave to silver.

In our Montana home, however, we use silver every day and polish it about twice a year. It's another of the little pleasures that come with country living.

The Steak Knife
Steel: Stainless, stainless alloy.
Length: Blade 4 to 5 inches, 8 to 9 inches overall.
Tip: Long clip, rigging, rounded.
Spine: Medium, medium stiff.
Blade bevel: Flat, V grind, or dropped V grind.
Edge bevel: Scalloped or serrated edge, 30 to 36 degrees.
Handle: Pakkawood, synthetic, wood, bone.
General information: Steak knives are excellent cutting utensils for any
    kind of sinewy meat. The blades on these knives are designed to
    cut, while the flat on a table knife does little more than pin tough
    meat to the plate so you can tear it apart with a fork.

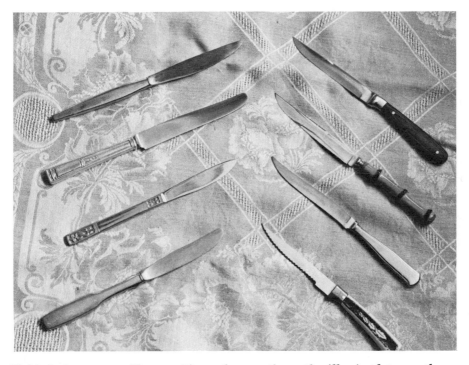

Table knives pose a dilemma. If you sharpen them, they'll ruin plates, so they have only minimal edging. (Steak knives: Coast Cutlery, Anton Wingen, Capri, Regent Sheffield. Butter knives: NA, Custom Craft, Anton Wingen, NA)

The most useful steak knife I've seen had a scalloped edge, a 4-inch medium-limber blade, and a rounded tip. There's no real need for a point on a steak knife, and the rounded tip made it a practical tool for slabbing and spreading butter. This knife was, however, capable of scratching fine china. If this is a concern of yours, choose an unsharpened edge with fine serrations along the first third of the knife blade. The straight part of the edge may be double-beveled to 36 to 42 degrees. This bevel is sharp enough to cut meat, and, because of its position on the blade, this section of the knife virtually never comes into hard cutting contact with a plate.

Part IV

Shop and Garden Knives

"Knife" is perhaps an awkward term to use for these tools, for very few of them have classic knife lines with an edge that parallels the length of the blade, a sharp point, and so forth. But they are nonetheless cutting instruments and rate as even greater workhorses than heavy outdoor knives. They must withstand tremendous impact; chisels are pounded with a mallet, and axes and machetes strike with hundreds of pounds of kinetic energy. They must also hold an edge while cutting wood, which is a much more durable material than those which food or outdoor knives usually come up against.

Because they must be tough, most shop and garden knives are fashioned from carbon steel alloys. Their bevels are also less acute in order to put more steel and strength behind the cutting edge. Too, many are sharpened differently than are standard knives; their edges don't require polishing, and beveling may be done with files or high-speed tool grinders. In addition, the blade bevel and edge bevel are often one.

For purposes of this discussion, let's define shop knives as construction tools and garden knives as tools you would use for outdoor work. There is some crossover, but it's a workable division. Utility pocketknives find plenty of application in both places, so they're discussed as a third class.

SHOP KNIVES

Wood Shavers

  Planes and drawknives are used to shave wood. They don't cut deeply into the wood; rather, they remove thin shards with each stroke. Drawknives are the most difficult to control because they lack any sort of guard or gauge, but they remove the most wood with the least amount of effort. For most rough work drawknives are best; planes are used for fine finishing.

Drawknives
Steel: Straight carbon, carbon alloy.
Length: Blade 12 to 14 inches.
Tip: None.
Spine: Stiff.
Blade bevel: Edge bevel; the same single-edge bevel, 30 to 36 degrees.
Handle: A drawknife has a handle on each end of the blade at right
   angles to the cutting edge. Synthetic or wood is the usual handle
   material.

A drawknife is controlled by altering the angle of the blade in
relation to the working surface. It is a useful woodworking tool, one
that is often overlooked by modern carpenters. (NA)

General information: The drawknife rates as something of an antique
among professional carpenters, but it is an excellent tool for rough
shop and yard work. It is perfect for peeling and pointing fence
posts and rungs; it will square up logs into timbers and carve curves
into dimensioned lumber.

The drawknife is used with the flat, unbeveled part of the blade
facing the wood. It shaves as the user pulls it toward him. The amount
of wood it removes with each stroke is determined by the angle of the
edge in relation to the working surface. That angle is controlled and
determined by the position of the handles. Hold the handles nearly
parallel to the surface to be cut, and you will shave off thin strips of
wood. Increase the angle between the blade and the working surface,
and you will peel off thicker strips of wood.

You will make the most controlled cuts if you hold the knife so the
spine of the blade is not at a right angle to the working surface. When
you hold the drawknife at a 42- to 60-degree angle, you impart a slicing
as well as a shaving action to the blade, and the cutting ability of the
edge becomes more efficient.

When a drawknife is used to peel logs, posts, and paint, it's sometimes easier to reverse the position of the blade so the bevel faces the
working surface. In this case the blade is held on a 36- to 42-degree
angle to the wood. This trick works best when the bark is wet (either
green or soaked with water) or the paint has been softened with paint
remover.

Planes
Steel: Straight carbon, carbon alloy.
Length: 1 to 4 inches of edge, 4 to 8 inches of blade.
Tip: Square.
Spine: Stiff.
Blade and edge bevels: 30 to 36 degrees, single-edge bevel.
Handle: Synthetic, wood.
General information: Planes consist of a sharp leading edge that juts
from a sliding face of smooth steel. The blade is locked in place by
an adjustable finger bolt, so there's no room for the slippage and
human error common to drawknives. Planes are finishing tools
that remove small but perfectly measured strips of wood shavings
with each stroke.

The two most common mistakes made with a plane (aside from

*Planes are precision instruments that remove
equal strips of wood with each stroke. (Stanley)*

using a dull blade) are trying to take too thick a shaving with each swipe, which clogs the blade so that the plane skips, and failing to keep the blade edge at a 42- to 60-degree angle to the direction of the cut, as one would with a drawknife, thus causing the plane to dig out chunks of wood rather than an even strip.

There are exceptions, but it's generally best to go with the grain of the wood. If you go against the grain, the blade digs deep and clogs. Planes will work across grain, but you must first bevel 90-degree corners to 45 degrees, or you'll tear splinters from the edge.

A handy trick to remember when you're using a plane is to polish the face of the tool with steel wool to make it glassy smooth. This lets it slide more easily. You can make it even slicker by waxing and buffing it.

Carpenter's Knife

Steel: Carbon alloy, stainless alloy.

Length: Blade 3 to 4 inches.

Tip: Coping, sheep foot, spear.

Spine: Stiff.

Blade bevel: V or flat ground.

Edge bevel: Double edge, 24 to 30 degrees.

Handle: Synthetic, wood.

General information: A whittling knife may be one piece or a folder, though you'll probably find a folder more convenient. It's extremely useful when you're doing detailed work with 1 inch thick or less of wood stock.

    The kinds of jobs it does include trimming stubborn sills and frames to fit and coping out corner and ceiling moldings. When trimming long edges, use this knife like a small drawknife, with both hands for control as you draw the edge to you. Work with the grain—and don't remove too much wood at one time.

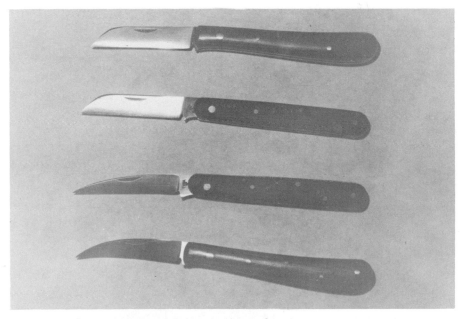

The carpenter's knife is a whittling knife used to score and shave wood. This blade also makes an excellent garden knife for budding, grafting, and light pruning. (Tina)

For coping, cut against a stable surface, bringing the most pressure to bear with your thumb on the spine of the knife. Score the cut to be made with the tip of the knife, then use the edge to cut and peel away wood.

If you end up with a slightly rounded cut that doesn't fit flush, you can flatten it with a wood block and sandpaper.

WOOD CHISELS

Chisels and gouges are used to chip, cut, and carve out niches and blocks from a flat surface of wood. They should be struck on the butt by the palm of your hand for shallow cuts and by a leather or wooden mallet for deep cuts. The size of the cut determines the size of the blade to use. The greater the width of wood you must remove, the wider the blade you should choose.

Chisels
Steel: Straight carbon, carbon alloy.
Length: Blade 4 to 5 inches; edges ¼, ½, 1, 1½, and 2 inches. These
    five chisel sizes will suffice for most home shop work.
Tip: Square.
Spine: Stiff.
Blade and edge bevels: 30 to 36 degrees, single-edge bevel.

Chisels cut at the tip and come in different widths
to match the size of the cut you must make. High-impact
synthetic handles are the most durable. (Shark-o-Lite)

Handle: High impact synthetic, or wood with full tang and pommel.

General information: The single-edge bevel on a chisel is the clue to using the tool. When you chisel with the beveled side up, the edge digs into the wood and cuts deep and fast. Chisel with the bevel side down; by altering the angle of the blade and handle to the wood, you can remove uniform strips of wood from a thin shaving to a thick shard.

When you are cutting straight down with a chisel, as would be necessary to seat a door latch, the beveled side of the blade should face the interior of the seat. Reversing the blade would result in sloping, rather than straight, sides. Chisels may also be used to make cutouts in plywood or composition wallboard for things like electrical outlets.

Gouges

Steel: Straight carbon, carbon alloy.

Length: Blade 3 to 5 inches; cutting edge ⅛ to 1½ inches.

Tip: The tip of a gouge is bellied to form a V or a U.

Spine: Stiff.

Blade and edge bevels: 30 to 36 degrees, single-edge bevel.

Handle: High-impact synthetic. Wood acceptable on ⅛- to ¼-inch tips.

General information: The bellied tip of a gouge acts like a scoop to dig out wood. It is controlled the same way as a chisel. A gouge

Gouges are used to hollow out rounded interiors from solid blocks of wood. Variations on gouge-tip conformation are also useful as artists' tools for such projects as making woodcuts and carving decoys. (Craftsman)

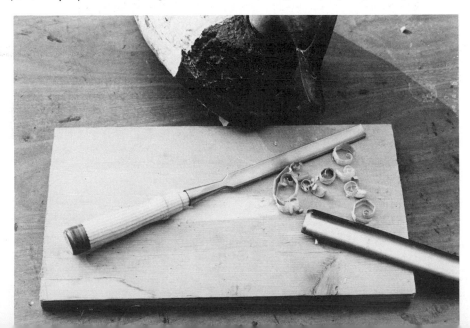

is used for such jobs as making slides and tracks for doors and drawers, and for artistic pursuits like carving woodcuts or ornamental duck decoys. It may also be used in lieu of a drill to cut holes in up to 1-inch stock.

Straight-Edge Cutters

This class of shop knife is characterized by a blade that does most of its cutting work at the tip. It is normally used in conjunction with some sort of guide, like the hard steel edge of a carpenter's square. The blade tip is held firmly against and aligned with the guiding edge, then drawn across the material to be cut, which in turn is backed by a hard, flat surface.

Typical work for this blade design is cutting pasteboard, linoleum, floor and ceiling tiles, wallpaper, and wood stripping.

Linoleum Knife
Steel: Straight carbon, carbon alloy.
Length: Blade 3 to 5 inches, 7 to 9 inches overall.
Tip: Pruning.
Spine: Medium.
Blade bevel: Flat ground.
Edge bevel: V grind, double edge, 18 to 24 degrees.
Handle: Wood, synthetic.
General information: A linoleum knife, with its pruning tip, offers the
    dual advantage of a cutting tip and a highly efficient cutting edge.
    It is most practically employed on soft, supple materials like lino-
    leum, tarpaper, and asphalt roofing.

The initial tip cut, made on a flat surface and directed by a straight edge, should constitute only one stroke. This scores the material but does not always cut it through. To complete the cut, the material is creased at the score and the knife reversed, so the point juts upward. The rounded, inside edge of the pruning tip now completes the slice, cutting from the bottom up. The pruning tip is most efficient at this job, because gravity and resistance increase the cutting ability of the edge as the material rides up toward the tip. A straight-edged blade would require either several successive cuts or an awkward, hard-to-control position for your hand.

It's extremely important to keep the tip of a linoleum knife clean and smooth. You'll find when cutting most roofing materials that the

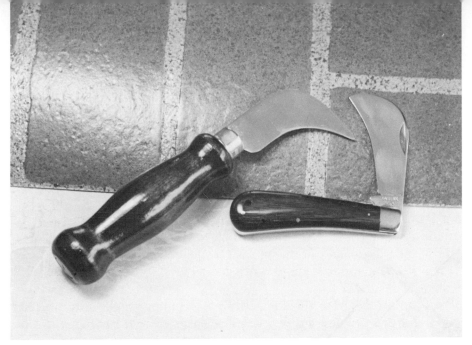

*Linoleum knives score at the tip, then slice from the
reverse side. As the material to be cut rides up on the sharpened
inside edge, gravity and friction aid in the cutting process. The
pruning tip on these knives is also useful for working in the
garden and for stripping electrical wires. (Hyde, Case)*

tip will tend to get clogged with tar. Clean this gunk off regularly with
lighter fluid or paint thinner; otherwise, it will be impossible to get
a deep, clean score.

Pasteboard Knife
Steel: Straight carbon, carbon alloy.
Length: Blade 1 to 3 inches, 4 to 6 inches overall.
Tip: Coping, sheep foot.
Spine: Medium
Blade bevel: Flat ground.
Edge bevel: V, hollow, or concave grind, 18 to 24 degrees.
Handle: Synthetic, steel, wood.
General information: The pasteboard knife is used to cut all varieties
 of paper materials (wallpaper, hardboard, ceiling tile, etc.), and it
 is also capable of fine trimming work on softwoods. It differs from
 a linoleum knife in that all cutting work is done at the very tip.
  For a truly clean, professional-looking cut, the slice should be com-
pleted in one stroke—hence the need for razor sharpness. An interesting

variation of the pasteboard knife is a two-piece handle into which a single-edge razor blade is inserted. When the edge dulls, you reverse the blade. When that portion of the blade dulls, you throw out the old and slide in a new razor blade.

While the whittling knife, linoleum knife, and pasteboard knife have been discussed as separate entities, don't overlook the possibility of having all three blades and capabilities packed into one pocket folder.

YARD AND GARDEN KNIVES

Axes

Axes are not the efficient cutting tools most people imagine them to be. Jobs like cutting up firewood and cutting down trees are far more easily done with a saw. However, there are some individual ax types that are perfect for jobs homeowners and gardeners are often confronted with. In their proper capacity, they're invaluable tools.

Double-Bitted Ax
Steel: Straight carbon, carbon alloy.
Head weight: 3 to 5 pounds.
Head shape: The double-bitted ax has a sharpened edge on each side of the head.

Two types of axes that have been around for a long time: the double-bitted and single-bitted ax. Although axes are persistently popular, they really have limited cutting ability. (NA, NA)

Edge bevel: The cutting edge should be sharpened to 30 degrees. The splitting edge should be sharpened to 42 to 48 degrees. Both are double-beveled or cannel.

General information: In the days when loggers cut down trees with axes, the double-bitted ax was advantageous in that it didn't have to be sharpened as often as a single-edged ax. These days, however, the double-bit makes more sense as a two-in-one ax, with one edge for cutting and the other for splitting. The wide, 48-degree bevel is the splitting side of the head; the flare in the edge wedges a sawed log apart when you strike a butt end, making for better-burning firewood than a full log.

Because of its dual-purpose nature, the double-bitted ax also makes a good camp ax, though here again you'll find that many of the traditional jobs for axes are more efficiently done with a small camp saw.

Single-Bitted Ax

Steel: Straight carbon, carbon alloy.

Head weight: 3 to 5 pounds.

Head shape: Sharpened edge on one side of the head, flat butt on the other.

Edge bevel: 30 to 48 degrees, double-beveled or cannel.

General information: The single-bitted ax was designed to function as both a cutting tool and a hammer. Such versatility isn't really needed today, and when this ax is used as a hammer, its exposed edge poses some danger. The single-bitted ax is useful as a wood splitter in that the flattened back of the head can be struck with a sledge. Often, a splitting stroke won't cleave the wood cleanly. The edge gets buried and the head becomes stuck. With a single-bitted ax, you can continue to drive the edge deeper with a sledge hammer, the ax head now working like a wedge.

When you use any ax extensively, the head sometimes wobbles on the handle. This is dangerous, since the head could conceivably fly off. You can firm up the head rock-solid if you immerse the head and upper handle in a bucket of water overnight.

Maul Ax

Steel: Straight carbon, carbon alloy.

Head weight: 6 to 8 pounds.

Head shape: Sharpened edge on one side of the head, flat butt on the other.

The maul ax (right) combines the features of a sledgehammer and a wedge. It is the best wood-splitter of all the axes, capable of cleaving a 12-inch log in one blow. (Split King)

Edge bevel: 42 to 48 degrees, cannel or double-beveled.

General information: The maul ax is strictly a splitting ax for home firewood, but it is the master of this job, capable of cleaving a foot-thick oak log in one stroke. The heavy head weight, the unusually wide bevel, and the fast-tapering blade combine to wrench wood apart.

Like the single-bitted ax, the maul ax may be used as a wedge by striking the flattened back with a sledge.

The maul ax is the best head to choose for splitting, but whatever type you choose you'll find this chore a lot easier if you give the handle a little twist just as the edge strikes the wood. Don't do it too soon; you'll either hit the log butt with the flat of the blade and sting your hands, or find yourself on the end of a wild, deflected blow and a potentially dangerous situation. But executed correctly, that little twist will increase the ax's wedging effect, and firewood will literally fly apart.

Hudson Bay Ax

Steel: Straight carbon, carbon alloy.

Headweight: 2½ to 3 pounds.

Head shape: A single-bitted ax that tapers rapidly from cutting edge to flattened back.

Edge bevel: 30 to 36 degrees, double edge.

The Hudson Bay ax was an invaluable tool to Northwoodsmen because it was capable of so many jobs, but its varied talents are more capably performed by specialized ax designs. (Herter)

General information: The Hudson Bay ax, the most versatile of all the ax designs, is a light utility ax capable of a host of shop and home chores, from splitting small firewood to hammering spikes. It was standard equipment for trappers and wilderness wanderers of years past, who used this tool alone to build crude cabins and even the furnishings inside. (See also "Camping Knives," pages 90–93.)

Broadax
Steel: Straight carbon, carbon alloy.
Head weight: 4 to 8 pounds.
Head shape: A single-bitted ax with an extremely large edge area (hence the word "broad") tapering to a flattened back. Either the blade or handle on a broadax is canted.
Edge bevel: 24 to 30 degrees, single bevel.

Three antique axes that are still useful today: a two-handed broadax, a one-handed broadax, and an adze. (NA, NA, NA)

*After initial surf cuts, the broadax shaves logs into
a square timber. Broadaxes and adzes are indispensable
tools for building a log cabin and may be used to create the
rough-hewn timbers popular in modern open-beam ceilings.*

General information: The broadax is something of an antique today.
Heads came in a wide range of sizes and weights from two-handed
axes to hatchets. This was one of the primary tools of the frontier,
and was used to shape square building beams from logs.

The procedure first required the use of some sort of straightedge
to establish true dimensions. Most commonly, a chalked line was employed. When drawn bowstring-tight and plucked, the chalk-impreg-
nated twine left a straight line on the wood. Surf cuts were then made
along the log down to the chalkline. The broadax then took over, its
single-edge bevel chipping away and squaring the timber. The canted
blade or handle kept the widened back away from the work, affording a
straighter, smoother cut.

The broadax wasn't swung with the powerful stroke it takes to chop
a tree; rather, it was dropped for added accuracy. Gravity, not muscle
power, did the cutting.

Adze

Steel: Straight carbon, carbon alloy.

Head weight: 1½ to 6 pounds.

Head shape: A single-bitted ax with the edge fashioned at right angles, rather than parallel to the handle.

Edge bevel: 24 to 30 degrees, single edge.

General information: The adze was used for the same purpose as a broadax: to shape and square up timbers. It was dropped, not swung; but it differs from the broadax in that you straddled the timber with it and shaved it smooth from above. The adze requires slightly less savvy and accuracy than a broadax.

Although both tools are essentially objects of antiquity, I've got a hunch they'd be in greater demand if more people knew of their purpose—and their usefulness. An adze and a broadax were invaluable to us when we built our log cabin, and they have a use even in citified conditions. They are *the* tools for creating those rough-hewn timbers so popular today in open-beam ceilings.

Brush Ax

Steel: Straight carbon, carbon alloy.

Head weight: 4 to 5 pounds.

Head shape: Elongated cutting edge on one side with a hook at the tip. Viewed in profile, the brush ax (also called a brush hook) looks like a large linoleum or pruning knife affixed to an ax handle.

Edge bevel: 30 to 36 degrees, double edge.

General information: This is the ax to use when you have to clear brush. It is capable of cutting trees up to 3 inches in diameter with one stroke.

The hooked point of the ax head acts like a guard. When you clear brush, it's best to lop off trunks right next to the ground. With a conventional ax, a clean-cutting swing would carry the head through the wood and the edge would strike the ground, dulling quickly because of contact with rocks and other abrasive materials. The brush ax point strikes the ground first, arresting the downward motion of the head and protecting the sharpened edge.

The inside curve of the hook is another important part of this tool. It works like a scythe on light brush like wild roses and bullbrier. Rather than chopping downward, you can swing the head across, sickling out large mats of brush with one stroke.

The brush ax is the perfect tool for trimming tree limbs and clearing brush up to 3 inches in diameter. The hook on the blade protects the sharp edge from rocks and ground contact. (Excelsior)

Hatchet

Steel: Straight carbon, carbon alloy.

Head weight: 1½ to 3 pounds.

Head shape: A scaled-down single-bitted ax with a sharpened edge opposite a flattened back. Occasionally, hatchet heads have a notch for pulling nails.

Edge bevel: 30 to 36 degrees, double edge.

General information: A hatchet is a useful hand tool because it combines the features of a hammer with a light-duty cutting edge. It is, however, strictly a tool for rough work. Typical jobs for a hatchet include pointing and pounding small stakes, splitting kindling wood, and trimming thumb-sized branches from the trunks of trees.

A good yardstick of efficiency for any ax- or hatchet-type tool is to use a head weight sufficient to cut through a piece of wood in no more than two strokes. If a hefty swing on each side of the log does not cut it cleanly, use a heavier ax or switch to a saw. As soon as you have to cut

A *carpenter's hatchet and camp hatchet. These tools are useful for rough wood work, pulling nails, and hammering.*

wedges with an ax, you're using more energy than would be expended with a sharp saw.

BRUSH KNIVES

Light brush and thick-stemmed weeds that infest backyards and gardens are most efficiently removed by long knives. A brush ax would also do the job, but swinging its heavy head requires energy that isn't really needed.

Machete
Steel: Straight carbon, carbon alloy.
Length: Blade 18 to 22 inches, 22 to 28 inches overall.
Tip: Rigging.
Spine: Medium stiff.
Blade bevel: Flat ground.
Edge bevel: 24 to 30 degrees, double edge.
Handle: Synthetic, wood.

The machete is useful for clearing light brush and thick, soft-stemmed weeds. (Merkuria)

General information: Machetes were originally used to clear soft, pulpy jungle plants. They are comparatively light in weight, and consequently they aren't suited to larger woody stems. As a kind of geographical rule of thumb, I've found machetes best suited for light brush-clearing in the southern and southwestern United States.

To use a machete most efficiently, you should stroke in an arc, first angling the blade down toward the material to be cut, then curving it across the brush. At this point most of the cutting is done; end the stroke with the blade angling upward. Most of a machete's cutting capabilities lie in the front third of the blade, so keep this area especially sharp.

Bolo Knife
Steel: Straight carbon, carbon alloy.
Length: Blade 18 to 22 inches, 22 to 28 inches overall.
Tip: Scimitar.
Spine: Stiff.
Blade bevel: Flat ground.
Edge bevel: Rolled or V grind, double edge, 24 to 30 degrees.
Handle: Wood, synthetic.

The bolo knife has a heavy, curved blade. Its weight makes it a good tool for clearing brush up to thumb thickness. (NA)

General information: Bolo knives originated in the Philippines. They are a much heavier knife than the machete and so are suited to cutting heavier, tougher brush. They are capable of the same cutting duties as a hatchet—they can trim hardwood saplings up to thumb thickness. They are more efficient than a hatchet in clearing brush because of their extensive edge area. Bolo knives are used like machetes, with the cutting swing of their blade describing an arc.

UTILITY POCKETKNIVES

A pocket folder is a valuable tool for gardening and general handiwork. The jobs to which individual knives are suited are determined by the shape of their blades and by the relationship of those blades to one another. For example, a pruning blade would be a useless adjunct on a stockman's knife. There's simply no use for such a blade on the range. A pruning blade could, however, be usefully included in a pocketknife you would use for gardening and house repair chores. By definition, the blade is suited to pruning, but it's also useful for cutting linoleum, stripping electrical wires, and cleaning the interior burr from fresh-cut plastic and copper plumbing pipe.

There are a dozen basic blades that could conceivably be included in a utility pocketknife. My term "basic" excludes things like corkscrews, scissors, and spoons—but even with those limitations the possible combinations are endless. So, rather than listing patterns and combinations of blades, it's better first to examine blade shapes and the work they'll do. Once you understand this, you'll be in a position to select a knife with individual blades that have some relationship to each other and are suited to the jobs you plan to tackle. If you look hard enough and long enough, you'll be able to find a manufacturer that puts together just the combination of blades that suits your needs.

• The spear blade is the most common master blade on multiple-bladed folders. It is capable of doing a hundred house and garden chores, from budding and cutting flowers to stripping wire, but it is primarily designed for wood whittling and light cutting. A spear blade belongs on a knife that qualifies as "pocket stuff"—a general utility tool that is there when you need it to cut cord, sharpen a pencil, or slice open a reinforced cardboard box.

This needle-blade (on the wallet) and pen-blade combination is the perfect knife for a businessman. Its small 2½-inch frame can be carried unnoticed in a pocket, and the blades will do a multiplicity of daily cutting work: opening mail and cardboard boxes, cutting cord, sharpening pencils, and cleaning out the bowl of a pipe. (Case)

• The pen blade is second only to the spear as a popular companion to a folding knife. It is actually a scaled-down spear and, as such, rates as a mini-whittler. In fact, that was the origin of the design. The "penknife" was a small folder used to keep quill pens sharp. Like the spear, it is useful for very light cutting and does an excellent job in cleaning out the bowl of a pipe.

• The clip blade has a point which can be inserted into most material with relative ease; this blade is also capable of slicing and whittling. It is the most versatile of all the blades, so it is a standard blade on a pocketknife that's carried extensively in the out-of-doors. The clip blade is not a panacea, however. Other blade shapes do specific jobs better. This jack-of-all-trades, incidentally, is the master blade on that class of folders known as jackknives.

• The long clip is usually a long blade that sacrifices whittling control for point penetration. It's most commonly associated with pocketknives used for fishing or trapping.

*A typical rancher/stockman's knife. This blade combination
is useful in veterinary work and ranch cutting chores. It.
also makes a good carpenter's knife and is capable of
grafting, budding, and light pruning in the garden. (Queen)*

*The large sheep-foot blade on this congress pattern is a valuable asset to
a carpenter. It will shave wood, cope molding, and cut pasteboard.
The smaller clip blade adds to the general utility of this combination.
The congress pattern is also a good combination for electricians
and plumbers, and especially for work in the garden. (Queen)*

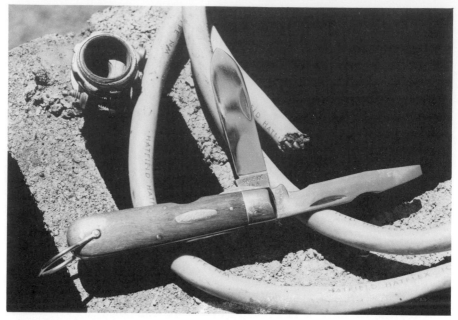

This spear/screwdriver combination makes an excellent pocketknife for handymen of all persuasions. The screwdriver/wire-stripper blade is worthy of special note in that it locks firmly in the open position. (Case)

The durable Boy Scout pattern is a classic design that has been standard pocket equipment for generations. It's more than "kid stuff," though; it has endured because of its tremendous utility as a spear (main blade), can opener, awl, and bottle opener/screwdriver. (Ulster)

This four-blade combination classifies as a true working knife. It's an ideal pattern for the carpenter and whittler, the plumber, and the electrician, and it makes an excellent budding, grafting, and light pruning knife as well. (Case)

If you're an outdoorsman as well as a do-it-yourselfer, this trapper/stockman pattern makes for a good compromise. The spey/long-clip-blade combination is capable of many building chores, and afield this knife may be used to clean fish, skin small game, and cape out trophy heads. (Case)

This is a mariner's knife, used for rope rigging. The sheep-foot blade makes for a good rope-cutter, and the round awl is used to tease twists of rope apart for splicing. (Old Timer)

• The saber shape provides penetration, strength, and slicing control at the tip. It's a short, sturdy blade, well suited to heavy cutting work: baring wires, cutting plastic pipe and hose, and cutting straight edges.

• The spey blade is actually a scalpel. It is one of the blades housed in the frame of farmers' and ranchers' pocketknives, used most often to castrate young pigs, sheep, and cattle. The spey also performs a variety of light tip-slicing chores, from cutting ceiling tiles to taxidermy work.

• The sheep-foot shape is favored for gardening. It is used to bud plants, to make grafts, and to cut flowers and vegetables. Flower stems should always be cut on a bias; hence, a knife, and not shears, must be used. This blade is also a good straight-edge cutter, useful on paper products and linoleum and around electrical wires and plumbing work.

• The coping blade is a tip-cutting whittling design, capable of fine wood-carving detail. The tip-cutting control also makes this a useful blade for gardening, farming, and straight-edge cutting. It is also a favorite of seamen; this design is perfectly suited to clean-slicing heavy ropes and rigging.

• The rigging tip is another favorite of those who work frequently with rope. With the point in line with the knife back, there is tight control at the tip, which is necessary when the tip is used like an awl to tease apart twists of rope before the rope is spliced. The rigging point is also useful when hunting or camping.

• The pruning tip, with its curved inside edge, is perfect for slicing suckers from fruit trees and ornamental shrubbery, cutting flowers, and light tree-and-shrub trimming. It is also the blade for heavy-duty straight-edge cutting—floor tiles, roofing tiles, and tarpaper—and has proved to be a useful tool for electricians and plumbers.

• The awl can be one of two designs. The leather awl is identified by a sharp point and a sharpened edge. It is roughly comparable to a very large needle in the work it will do, and consequently it is a common blade on pocketknives for outdoorsmen. In a pinch it provides a means to sew or otherwise bind together a host of heavy materials, from webbed belting to the torn floor of a life raft or ripped stitching on a pair of saddlebags. The rope awl is pointed and rounded, like a thick ice pick. It is used by mariners to tease apart twists of rope for splicing.

• The screwdriver isn't exactly a knife blade, but it's an invaluable asset on a pocketknife carried by a handyman. The screwdriver blade shouldn't be used when a real screwdriver is within reach; constant tightening of screws puts a lot of strain on the bolster. But there will be many times when a standard screwdriver is far from easy reach, and you'll bless the convenience of that blade on your knife. It will also be responsible for doing important work that otherwise would probably remain undone. When you notice a loose table leg or shaky doorlatch, the walk down to the shop for a screwdriver usually discourages prompt repair. You file it in your memory for Saturday morning—and usually forget it. With this blade on your knife, you have no excuse not to tighten that screw immediately.

Part V

Knife Care

IF YOU HAVE READ UP TO THIS POINT, you've digested some 35,000 words dedicated to choosing the right cutting tool for the work you have to do and using that tool in a craftsmanlike manner. All that reading will be worthless unless you read on, for you still have only half the knowledge you need.

This equipment is sufficient to sharpen most edges: a double-grit corundum stone, a "soft" Arkansas stone, a benchstone of aluminum oxide, and a razor strop. (Craftsman, Case, Case, Shell)

Any blade, excluding King Arthur's legendary sword, is going to dull with use. Knives that supposedly "stay sharp forever" are as mythical as Excalibur—unless, of course, they're never used. And if your knife is dull, no matter how carefully you've chosen its design and the material from which it's made, it will be useless as a tool. As a matter of fact it just may be in that condition when it's brand, shiny new. The vast majority of commercial cutlery arrives at the dealer with a "honed" edge. For all practical purposes, it is an edge that's merely ground onto the blade with a fine-grit stone and never polished. A honed edge, as you'll soon see, is just the first step in sharpening a knife to its ultimate efficiency.

THE "I-CAN'T-SHARPEN-A-KNIFE" SYNDROME

It would be a conservative guess that 75 percent of us can't sharpen a knife. Usually those who can't have some sort of mystic approach to their inability; they think that honing an edge is some kind of gift of the gods that was never bestowed upon them.

This is hardly the case. I've taught dozens of non-knife-sharpeners how to get a shaving edge in five minutes' time. Basically, the "I can't-sharpen-a-knife" syndrome is either a matter of ignorance or misinformation. You never learned how it was done, or someone taught you improperly.

I must admit in the same breath, however, that I have met a tiny minority of individuals who have a great deal of difficulty in trying to sharpen a knife. Their difficulty was so great, even with careful explanations and instruction, that I too began to wonder about those mystic implications—until I ran across the pet postulate of Bob Farquharson, vice-president of Case Cutlery. Bob's contention was that some people have such an unsteady hand that they find it nearly impossible to hold a blade at a regular angle and move their hand at the same time. In their grasp, the angle of the blade to the stone wavers and skips, creating a microscopic pattern of hills, rills, and valleys when there should be a straight, smooth plane honed on the edge.

His theory seems to work, for, operating under that assumption, I devised a way to counter the tendency to waver, and, using this simple trick, I have yet to find anyone who can't hone a shaving edge. I'll explain more about that in a moment, but my point is this: *anyone* can sharpen a knife.

THE KNIFE-SHARPENING PROCESS

Creating a sharp edge requires two distinct steps. The first step is beveling; the second is polishing. Note that in both steps, we are dealing only with the *edge bevel*. For all practical purposes, the blade bevel is a permanent, unalterable part of the knife blade.

A knife may not be sufficiently dull to warrant beveling but, for our purposes here, let's assume we're starting with a blade as dull as a butter knife. The purpose of this initial beveling process is to grind a perfect V into an edge that under a strong magnifying glass would resemble a U or a flattened surface if seen in cross section.

When beveling a blade, you have to remove some steel. It is rough work, exacting only to the extent that you have to maintain a regular angle of blade-to-stone, so the faster you remove that steel, the better. There are a whole host of devices used to accomplish this purpose, so before we start honing it might be worth looking at their individual merits.

Mechanized Grinders

• High-speed tool grinders amount to a whirling, abrasive stone. They are unquestionably the quickest, most efficient way to achieve a bevel, but they are difficult tools to control in the hands of a novice. They grind so quickly that they will remove uneven chunks from the cutting edge unless you keep the blade moving across the stone. Moving the blade *and* maintaining a perfect angle orientation is no small trick. There is also a danger that the friction resulting from high-speed grinding will heat up your blade to the tempering point. If your blade turns blue, you've lost the perfect temper initially imparted to the knife as well as a good deal of its worth.

• Kitchen knife sharpeners are baby brothers to tool grinders. They usually operate by way of two opposing grinding wheels, one turning clockwise, the other counterclockwise. Unless you move the knife back and forth smoothly over the whirling wheels, you'll tear out the same uneven chunks that a tool grinder will. Kitchen grinders don't go as fast as tool grinders, so retempering is less likely (though still possible). The main fault I find with these gadgets is that they lock you into one edge bevel for all knives (30 to 36 degrees on most of them), and the sharpening spectrum of kitchen knives varies between 18 and 48 degrees.

• Oil- or water-bath grinders revolve in a reservoir of liquid. The liquid keeps the pores of the stone clean and keeps the knife blade cool. They turn slowly, so there is less likelihood of an uneven edge, yet they are abrasive enough to bevel the aforementioned butter knife in a minute or so. They are my favorite for mechanized beveling.

Files

A fine-toothed file is an efficient tool for removing steel—more so than a stationary stone—but unless you have a large enough blade to clamp in a vise (ax, machete, et al.) you will find it impossible to maintain a regular angle orientation. Holding the blade in one hand and working a file with the other allows too much angle variation to be accurate.

Hand Stones

The most efficient hand stones for beveling will have a relatively coarse grit, comparable to heavy sand. Actually, these are usually not natural stones but composite abrasives: a brick of corundum, garnet, or hard oxide particles formed under titanic pressure.

A uniform edge bevel will be easiest to hone if you can cover the full distance of the edge—from hilt to tip—with each stroke; hence your stone should be about as long as the blade of the knife you're sharpening.

• Round stones usually come attached to some sort of handle. You

The trade name for this compressed aluminum oxide rod is Moon Stick. It may be used for touch-up like a steel, or for sharpening the hollows in a scalloped edge. The round-top stone is used to sharpen curved blades such as linoleum and pruning knives. (Case, Herman Wirth)

hold the knife in one hand and the stone in the other, and work one against the other, like a sharpening steel. While this beveling method looks and sounds effective with the comfortable *whishh-whishh-whishh* rhythm of stone against steel, it raises much the same problem as a file. With both beveling components in your hands, you get too much wobble for a perfectly beveled edge unless you're very much experienced at knife sharpening.

• Flat stones, because they lie solid and stationary as you work the knife steel against them, are the easiest sharpening medium to work with. The stone must have a perfectly flat surface. Old stones, or stones that have been misused, develop a contoured surface that imparts an uneven bevel. The most practical stones for price and performance have two grits, coarse on one side and fine on the other. The fine grit is used as the first polishing step, which we'll discuss later.

Keeping Hand Stones Clean

In order for hand stones to work most efficiently, they must be kept clean. This is true of all hand stones, including those used for polishing.

As you work steel against these stones, stone cuts steel—but steel also cuts stone. Your blade grinds off tiny dust-sized particles of grit that settle back on the stone. This does not happen with mechanized grinders. High-speed grinders and kitchen sharpeners spin the dust off. Oil- and water-bath grinders wash it off.

On a flat stone, however, the dust particles begin to clog the pores of the stone. This makes the surface of the stone smooth, so it doesn't cut with full efficiency. If your hands are sensitive, you'll be able to feel the slippage of blade against stone. A clean, fast-cutting stone has a slight drag to it, so you can feel the cutting process.

It follows that this residue must be cleaned off. Virtually every manufacturer or supplier of stones recommends that you use oil for this job, and I think they're on a par with people who once thought the earth was flat. There is no logic to back up their reasoning.

The notion is that the viscosity of oil will float the particles up and away from the pores of the stone. It might work if you had a constant bath of oil, as in a mechanized grinder, but a stone is flat, and corundum is one of the heavier minerals. It's one of the last to be sloughed off when you're panning for gold, which is one of the heaviest elements. Corundum is bound to sink, not float.

Then, too, no one is going to use a stone in an oil bath. You put a drop of oil on the stone and work it into the pores. Then another drop. And another drop. The net result is that shards of sharpening stone work down into the pores, clogging them in a gunky mass of oil and powder. Furthermore, oil is also a lubricant, so it encourages slippage over the stone rather than the drag which marks efficient cutting.

In short, I don't recommend using oil on a sharpening stone. The best liquid I've found to clean pores is plain hot water. As soon as drag begins to lessen, run the stone under water, rubbing it with your thumb, and watch the powder darken the sink. When it stops, the stone is clean and ready for more cutting. You may have to do this several times during the beveling of an extremely dull knife, but a trip to the sink will be less work in the long run than messing with oil.

If the stone is old and has already been used with oil, you'll probably have to free the pores with hot, soapy water and a hard scrubbing with a wire brush, then repeat the process after a few knives have been sharpened to leach the stone of residue oil. It's extra work, but it will be worth the effort.

Sharpening Strokes

There are three possible strokes to use on a flat stone when you're working on bevel. The most preferable is to sharpen the edge into the stone. It is not the quickest way, but it's great practice for the polishing to come.

Moving the blade in a circular motion requires the least energy and is the easiest way to control the angle of the blade in relation to the stone. This is the most efficient stroke for tools like chisels and planes, but with knives it tends to create an uneven grind where the edge pitches up to meet the tip.

Moving the edge away from the stone is the poorest sharpening technique. It is slow cutting and creates a rollover (a microscopically thin sheet of steel that trails from the edge and interferes with cutting, like an invisible cap over a keen blade).

This rollover also occurs when high-speed and oil-bath grinders are used. It must be removed before the polishing step, and this is done by moving the edge into a flat stone until the wisp of steel is eaten away.

Beginners will find beveling easiest if they lay the stone on a flat surface, such as a workbench, and control the angle and drift of the blade with both hands. Two hands firm up and maintain the blade-to-stone angle better than one.

Getting the Angle

The angle at which you hold the blade to the stone determines the type of bevel you'll hone, and the acuteness of that angle is a major component of that knife's performance. For example, if the edge bevel on a meat slicer is not acute enough, it will not be sharp enough to slice meat cleanly, and the blade will not perform its intended function. At the other extreme, a 24-degree bevel on an ax would crumble and nick under the impact of chopping.

The angle of edge bevel is determined by how far you raise the back or spine of the knife from the stone. Viewed from the side, the stone, edge, and back of the knife form a right-angled triangle. The edge bevel you eventually hone will be twice the number of degrees measured at the most acute angle (the place where the edge meets the stone).

If you're working on the standard double-edge or V bevel and you hold the blade at a 10-degree angle to the stone, you'll eventually hone a 20-degree bevel. A 15-degree angle would create a 30-degree bevel, and so on. The bevel is doubled because you hone a plane of steel into each side of the blade.

PENNY CHART & ANGLE RELATIONSHIP

PENNY THICKNESS	½" BLADE	1" BLADE	1½" BLADE	2" BLADE
1-PENNY	6°	3°	2°	1.5°
2-PENNY	12°	6°	4°	3°
3-PENNY	18°	9°	6°	4.5°
4-PENNY	24°	12°	8°	6°
5-PENNY	30°	15°	10°	7.5°

24° TOTAL EDGE BEVEL · ½" KNIFE BLADE · 12° BEVEL ON EACH SIDE · 2-PENNY THICKNESS · SHARPENING STONE

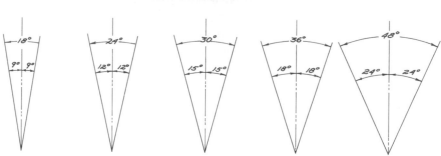

There are two ways to assure yourself of a proper bevel. The first is sight. Get a protractor and measure and draw the angle of bevel needed on the knife you're sharpening. Remember to divide by two when you're working with a V edge. Once you see the angle you'll need, you'll find it surprisingly easy to maintain your blade orientation to the stone by feel.

If you have trouble maintaining orientation freehand, try this: First, cut that protracted angle from a piece of posterboard and slide it be-

A regular angle of knife blade to stone is easy to maintain if you use your thumb like a gauge or spacer as the blade moves along.

tween the side of the blade and the stone until the point of the angle cutout reaches the edge of the knife. Now use your thumb to gauge the distance from the knife back to the stone. With the handle cradled in your palm, rest the bottom of your thumb on the knife back so the side of your thumb barely touches the stone. Your thumb now acts as a guide as the knife moves along.

When you first try this technique, you'll save time otherwise spent measuring each stroke if you'll mark your thumb with a ballpoint pen along the line where it meets the knife back.

Yet another method may be used if you "can't" sharpen a knife; this makes use of pennies instead of your thumb for a guide. Depending on the distance between knife edge and back, stack a number of pennies until their combined height creates the desired angle. Rest the knife back on the stack, and you have an infallible check on the proper angle. If you need the initial assurance, move the pennies

You can ascertain the angle at which you're sharpening a knife by using a protracted cutout as a check. An even easier way is via a stack of pennies.

with the blade as you sharpen; with the knife back so blocked, you can't deviate from that angle. Admittedly it's slow going at first, but if you keep your stone clean and cutting well, the penny method will bevel the dullest knife in four or five minutes. And with practice, and confidence in your ability to sharpen a knife, you'll soon be able to discard the pennies. The same thing will hold true if you choose to use your thumb for a guide. Your hand will become accustomed to the feel of a proper blade-to-stone orientation, and you'll be able to freehand an edge bevel to within five degrees of a perfect angle.

Getting the Bevel

Begin by laying the knife blade flat on the stone. Let's assume you want an edge in the neighborhood of 24 degrees. Remember that this angle takes in *both* bevels. You must therefore split the difference, honing an angle of approximately 12 degrees on each side of the blade. Tip the blade up so spine and edge lie at roughly a 12-degree angle to the face of the stone and start cutting.

As the blade moves against the stone, pay particular attention to

At the beginning of the sharpening stroke the edge should be at a perfect right angle to the stone.

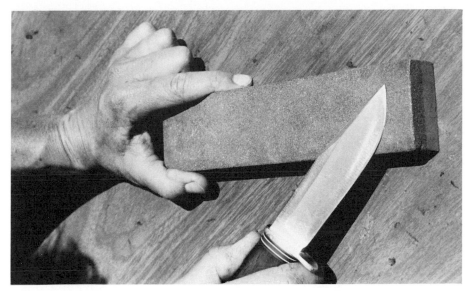

*As the edge is pushed forward, the relationship between the
back of the knife and the stone swings to a 45-degree angle to
include the rounded tip section in the sharpening stroke.*

uniformity. An equal amount of steel must be removed from all sections of the edge. This is easy enough to accomplish on the flat part of
the edge, but it is difficult on the upsweep as you near the point. If
you're beveling in a circular motion, make that motion more oval when
you get to the upsweep. If you're honing into the stone, begin to pivot
the knife when the upsweep strikes the stone. Remember that the *edge*
should always be as close to a right angle to the longest dimension of
the stone as is possible. As your knife pivots along the curved edge, the
angle relationship between spine and stone will change, but not the
relationship between edge and stone. On most knives the spine should
be at about a 45-degree angle to the stone at the end of the stroke which
is sharpening the very tip.

Removing an equal amount of steel from both sides of the blade
is just as important as overall uniformity of individual bevels. This is
yet another reason for moving an edge *into* the stone. Push the blade
away from you, flip it over, and pull it toward you. As a result, you
will have an equal number of sharpening strokes on each side of the
blade and, thus, matching bevels.

If you have cut your steel by any means other than by moving the
edge into the stone, the final process in the beveling step will be several

strokes into a flat stone, exactly as described above. Tool grinders, bath grinders, and circular sharpening all leave traces of rollover, and moving the edge into a stone is the only way to remove that rollover. Beveling a knife by moving it into a stone also aligns the microscopic edge scratches created by the coarse grit so that they are more easily removed during the polishing process.

When a knife is properly beveled, the edge should come to a perfect V from point to hilt. There are three ways to ascertain whether or not you have achieved that V. First, when you feel both sides of the knife dragging hard against the stone and hear a meaty, metallic *whish-h-h-h* as you stroke, you have probably achieved your bevel.

Second, hold the blade between you and a source of light, edge up, point toward you, and roll the handle upward and downward so light can reflect off the cutting edge of the knife. If you see any reflection, there is still some flatness in the edge, and you must bevel some more.

Finally, rest the cutting edge *lightly* on your thumbnail and slowly draw it across the full span of the edge. If the knife gently drags without any smooth slipping, you have a good bevel. If some portion of the blade slips, that section needs more work. Pay particular attention to the tip section of the knife. This is the part of the edge that is the most difficult to bevel properly.

A properly beveled edge, magnified several times. The angle from blade bevel to cutting edge is straight and uniform, and the face of the bevel is flat. Note, however, the deep scratches in the beveled surface. For a truly sharp edge, these must be removed by polishing.

All this description and advice may suggest that beveling in itself is a long labor of love. It isn't. In practiced hands, the process, beginning with an RC 58 carbon steel as dull as a butter knife, should take less than a minute on a flat stone—and thirty seconds with the aid of some sort of mechanized grinder.

Someone who has never sharpened a knife before and who pays careful attention to what he is doing will probably need five to seven minutes, and that time will decrease rapidly with experience.

Polishing the Edge

The polishing process, on paper at least, may appear equally complex and lengthy, but in practice it's just as fast and just as simple as beveling. It constitutes nothing more than stropping the bevel you've ground against a variety of textures, each finer, smoother, and less abrasive than the previous one. If you were to view your beveling job under a 20-power magnifying glass, you would see deep scratches on the bevel you've created and tiny sawteeth on the very edge. Polishing removes these scratches and makes the bevel mirror smooth, reducing the size of those sawteeth to a microscopic level. Here are the various steps involved in polishing:

• First, use a fine-grit composition stone (particles about the size of fine sand). You may substitute an oil- or water-bath grinder equipped with a fine abrasive grit, but the saving in energy is debatable. If you've honed a proper bevel, each polishing step will require no more than ten strokes per edge, and probably less.

If you used pennies or other aids to get a bevel, continue to use them for polishing, as this must be done at the same angle as beveling. Work the edge into the fine grit, and always work *into* the stone when polishing. Be sure to maintain equal contact with all parts of both edges. Remember, too, that the stone must be kept free of dust buildup. The fine grit corundum will have done its job when you begin to feel significant cutting drag, and when, upon close examination of the beveled edge, you see no deep scars or scratches from the coarse-grit stone. Another careful test you can make is to flick your thumb at right angles across the edge. If your skin seems to hang up and will not slide smoothly, you're finished with this step. Again, double-check the tip portion of the edge.

• The next grit in the polishing process is "Washita" or "soft

Arkansas" stone. This natural abrasive is quarried in the Ozarks and goes by the proper name of novaculite. Another suitable polishing stone is compressed aluminum oxide, a manmade composite stone formed under pressure like corundum.

The polishing procedure is identical to the step before. Maintain the precision of your angle and move into the stone. The feel as the blade gets sharper will be different, however. Blade resistance will be greatest at the beginning of your strokes. As the edge is polished, it will slide more easily across the face of the stone. When you feel no resistance, you've probably completed this part of the polishing process. Ten strokes to a side should be sufficient.

Because the grit on this stone is so fine, its pores clog easily, so you should clean this stone often. When it gets dirty, you can usually see a sheen or shine on the surface. When it is clean, novaculite or aluminum oxide appears flat, like wall paint.

There are two final tests for this step: (1) when you look closely at the bevel, it will have no scratches at all, just a dull luster; (2) when you scrape your thumbnail with the blade perpendicular to the nail, you should get light shavings of nail material. Do this ever so lightly. You should need little more pressure than the weight of the blade.

• "Hard Arkansas," "Arkansas white," or "bench stone" are three common names for the hardest form of novaculite. If you are a purist, whet the blade against this grit ten times. I'm not *that* much of a purist, so I usually skip this step with perfectly satisfactory results.

• Leather stropping comes next. The ideal tool for this is a razor strop. A razor strop has a coarse, woven-cloth-like side and a soft, smooth, unpolished leather side. Strop the knife *away* from the edge on the coarse side first, ten strokes on a side, then *away* from the edge on the leather side ten times. The coarse side occasionally needs cleaning with a washcloth and warm water. About once every fifty sharpenings it will need a washing. The leather needs oil to keep it from drying out. Neatsfoot oil works fine. Apply it when the leather feels dry to the touch.

If you can't locate a razor strop (they are practically antiques), the next best bet is a leather belt, so long as it does not have a hard, highly polished surface. The best belts will be natural leather, identified by a coarse, grainy side and a soft smooth side. Use these just like a razor strop: the rough side first, then the smooth side. If you can't locate such

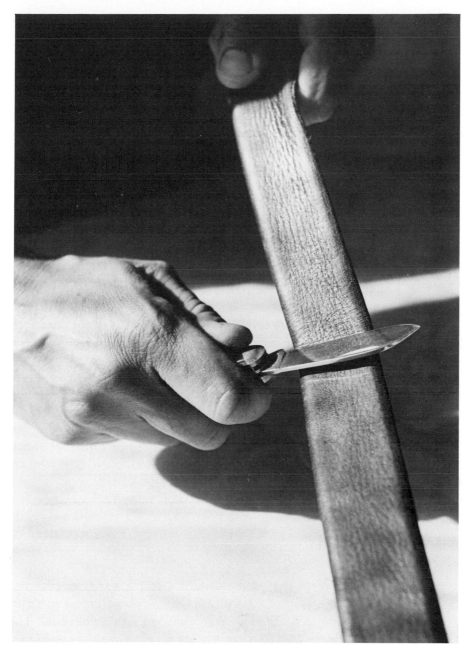

Leather razor strops are best for the final polishing step, but they are hard to find these days. A soft, natural leather belt is a good substitute. In a pinch, you may use the side of a boot or even a knife sheath.

a belt, virtually any natural leather will do this job; I have used an old boot and even a knife sheath as a strop at one time or another.

The final step is hand polishing. If you're the nervous type, you can skip it. Hand polishing is nothing more than working the edge over the palm of your hand ten to twenty times to a side. Obviously, you work away from the cutting edge here too. The oil of your hand, the abrasiveness of your dead surface skin, added to the tiny bits of grit your hand has picked up during the sharpening process, all combine to impart that last touch of brilliant keenness to the edge. After you've finished this step, a knife initially beveled at 24 degrees should easily shave hair.

Bevel Angles and Sharpening Steps

The sharpening process I've described might well be considered the ultimate sharpening. It is the way to achieve a shaving edge, that elusive badge of excellence sought by just about anyone who has ever picked up a knife.

But religiously following each of those polishing steps becomes nothing more than an exercise if the angle of the blade bevel becomes less acute. You could strop a 36-degree angle from now until Christmas and it would not shave a hair; the blade bevel isn't capable of such duty, even after polishing.

So, as a rule of thumb, subtract one sharpening step for each six degrees of angle added on to a shaving (24-degree) edge. For a 30-degree edge, you need go no further than polishing on a leather strop, a 36-degree edge will be "sharp" after a honing on novaculite, and so forth.

Knife Steels and Touch-ups

No matter what you're cutting with your blade, from soft bread to hardwood, the edge will eventually dull.

Once you become accustomed to the luxury and excellence of a truly sharp knife, you'll notice this dullness as you use the instrument. A sharp knife will set up a lot of drag as you slice, but you'll need virtually no downward pressure to make the cut. A dull knife will slide back and forth smoothly, but you'll have to exert more downward pressure to cut.

The more pressure you exert, the less control you have. Some of that loss of control will be evidenced in the lack of precision of your cut. A great deal of the loss of control will be evident—with possibly tragic consequences—if that dull blade slips off a roast or skids off the top of a turnip. This, incidentally, proves the claim that dull knives are more dangerous than sharp ones. The blade is indeed dull, but your compensating pressure makes up for its lack of cutting qualities. An edge perfectly capable of deep cutting is now essentially running wild with no guidance. What will stop it? A cutting board? Perhaps, but so might your thumb—or the person sitting next to you at dinner.

This same principle holds true for all cutting tools, from ax blades to chisels to hunting knives. So long as they are being used for the job they were designed to do, they are much safer when they are sharp.

When a properly sharpened knife first begins to dull, it need not be fully resharpened, from rebeveling through stropping. All it needs is a touch-up.

The easiest way to do this is with a knife steel. Knife steels are made with extremely high carbon content and are almost diamond hard. Their surface is roughened to a point where it is mildly abrasive. While there is no true grit on a steel, its abrasive qualities are a shade finer than those of novaculite. In fact, steels remove very little edge material as they sharpen. Their primary function is to realign the cutting edge.

In my description of the sharpening process, I mentioned that beveling creates sawteeth along the cutting edge. Successive polishing reduces the size of those sawteeth, but it doesn't eliminate them. Even a razor, at 15 to 18 degrees of edge bevel, would have very fine sawteeth if you viewed the edge under a powerful microscope. These teeth are unavoidable, and, in fact, they aid in cutting; but as you use the knife you force these tiny "teeth" out of alignment, creating a situation comparable to a rollover on a minute scale. A steel puts "teeth" back on the cutting edge and removes those that have rolled over. This, by the way, is why the best steels are magnetized. The magnetic effect holds the shards of steel and, to some extent, aids in realignment.

How often should a steel be used? When cutting meats, especially hot meats, I find that my knife needs a steel touch-up after about every five slices. Just two or three strokes of edge against steel is more than sufficient. And, like polishing steps, steels aren't particularly useful on knives with greater edge bevels than 30 degrees.

One thing steels are *not* are tools to sharpen dull knives. They are a means to touch up a properly-sharpened edge, not a sharpening device in and of themselves. When the stroke of a steel no longer returns an edge to keenness, it's time for the edge to be repolished. Note that I said r*epolishing*, not resharpening. Start with the novaculite or aluminum stone, then strop the edge with leather and polish it against your hand. The entire process should take about 30 seconds and should return a 24-degree bevel to shaving sharpness.

You can do this many times and still get your shaving edge back. Then, somewhere along the line, you won't be able to shave hair, even though you've carefully repolished the edge. What happened? The very edge of the blade—a tiny portion of the steel too small to be perceived by the naked eye—has taken on a new, less acute bevel from the many polishings. Remember, polishing removes steel from the blade just as beveling does, but in much smaller amounts.

To return the edge to razor sharpness, you must rebevel that small section of edge by going back to the fine-grit corundum, then following the rest of the polishing steps. Eventually, the bevel created by the fine-grit corundum will become less acute. Then you have to go back one step further and work with the coarse corundum—and so forth, until you ultimately reach a point where the entire bevel you once ground into the blade is so altered by successive polishings that it no longer has its original bevel. You cannot hone an edge on any blade that is more acute than the bevel. At this point, you must go back to the grinder or coarse-grit corundum and cut a new edge bevel into the meat of the blade, followed by all the polishing steps.

How often will each of these steps be required? I use knives a great deal, and for a great variety of jobs, so, as a rule of thumb, here's the amount of sharpening I have found necessary in a few representative categories:

• Butchering 100 pounds of steaks from a quarter of beef: frequent steeling, three touch-ups with an Arkansas stone followed by a sequence of fine-grit corundum, Arkansas stone, leather, and hand when I'm done so the knife will be sharp for the next butchering. Full rebeveling once a year. Total meat cut, around 1,500 pounds.

• Carving roasts: constant steeling, Arkansas-to-hand touch-up needed about every other meal. This is partially because carving table meat brings the edge in contact with bone often, and bone dulls a knife like stone. Back to beveling about once every six months.

• Fileting and cleaning fish: Frequent steeling, Arkansas-to-hand touch-up every 25 pounds of fish. Rebeveling about every 100 pounds of fish. Scales, skin, and cutting through bone by mistake (even though fish bones are soft) play havoc with an edge.

• Hunting knife (cleaning big game): Arkansas-to-leather routine after every deer. A similar touch-up halfway through the job of cleaning bigger elk and moose. Rebeveling about once every two years. Cleaning game is hard on a knife owing to the abrasive qualities of bone and hair, but the hunting season lasts only a month.

• Kitchen and cooking knives are impossible to fit into any rules of thumb because so much depends on what they're cutting. A chef's knife or vegetable parer, if it were used on such foods as peeled potatoes, cleaned celery, and lettuce, would probably last for a year without the need for a touch-up, and might never need rebeveling in your lifetime. But use a knife to cut highly acidic citrus fruits, or tomatoes, or to peel potatoes or carrots with dirt on their skins, and it will need touching up after each use. Similar variables occur in other aspects of use. Do you cut on a board or against sink porcelain or Formica? Are the knives stored where their edges can work against other steel utensils, or are their edges somehow protected?

Once you learn what a properly sharpened edge feels like and witness its effortless usage and precision accomplishments, you won't need rules of thumb. You'll keep and maintain sharp edges on all your cutting tools as a matter of habit and common sense.

SPECIAL SHARPENING TECHNIQUES

The aforementioned sharpening techniques apply to standard blades with a V-type edge bevel. Other edge types require slightly different techniques, though the polishing steps, from the coarsest to the finest grit, remain essentially the same.

Single-Edge Bevels

When honing a single-edge bevel, remember that the angle of blade to stone will be the angle of your edge. If you hold a chisel at a 30-degree angle to the stone, you will have a 30-degree edge bevel.

When honing a more acute edge than 30 degrees, always move the blade into the stone. When you wish an angle 30 degrees or greater you may move the blade in a circular motion for greater control and a perfectly flat edge bevel. This is most important with tools whose blade bevel and edge bevel are essentially one, like planes, chisels, and drawknives.

Never bevel the flat backside of a single-bevel blade. You may polish it lightly to promote smoothness, but do so with the blade perfectly flat.

Hollow and Concave Grinds

Because there is so little steel behind the cutting edge on a hollow or concave grind, these grinds are all too easily retempered and ground into unwanted scallops by high-speed or kitchen grinders. Even a coarse-grit hand stone cuts into the meat of these blades rapidly. Unless they are dull as a round rock, start the sharpening process at the fine-grit corundum stage and go slowly and carefully. This type of grind sharpens quickly and easily and that's the main reason for its popularity.

Scalloped Edges

Never buy a scalloped-edge knife with a double-scalloped edge— that is, one with an identical bevel ground into both sides of the knife.

When a scalloped edge has scallops ground from both sides of the blade, it is difficult to sharpen. Honing each scallop against a round stone will eventually get the job done, but it's tedious work. Roll-overs are particularly maddening, so always move a scalloped edge into the stone.

They are virtually impossible to sharpen. For a scalloped edge to be capable of being sharpened, it should have a perfectly flat single-edge bevel on one side of the knife. Since these bevels are often very acute —5 to 10 degrees—they may be hard to perceive, but they should be there.

There is only one way to sharpen these knives and that's by moving the single-edge bevel into a hand stone. Grinders of any kind, or any other sort of sharpening motion, will create a rollover inside the scallops that's maddening to try to remove.

The only way to remove that rollover (or to bevel a double-scalloped edge) is to move into each individual scallop with a round hand stone. They cannot be polished further.

Serrated Edges

If used properly, a serrated edge never needs resharpening. It rips and tears, rather than cutting in the classic sense, so a critical edge isn't required. There will be times, however, when someone tries to saw wood or bone with it. When the teeth no longer catch and skip as the edge is drawn lightly across a fingertip, it indicates that the tooth points are dull.

As with a scalloped edge, a serrated-edge knife must have only one bevel to be sharpened. Move this bevel into the stone. Individual teeth can't be resharpened.

Canneled Edge

The canneled edge is common on chopping tools like axes and cleavers. Instead of forming a flat edge bevel, the steel curves down to meet the cutting edge.

The most reliable way to put a canneled edge on a tool is with a file. Secure the tool to be sharpened to a solid surface with a clamp or vise, and roll the file as you work. Cut with the file in one direction only, from tip to handle. Filing in the reverse will flatten the fine teeth of the file and render it impotent.

High-speed grinders are also useful for sharpening heavy tools; there's a lot more steel to be removed than on a slender knife blade, and the blade surface absorbs the heat of grinding so there's little danger of improper tempering. Remember to roll the tool against the wheel.

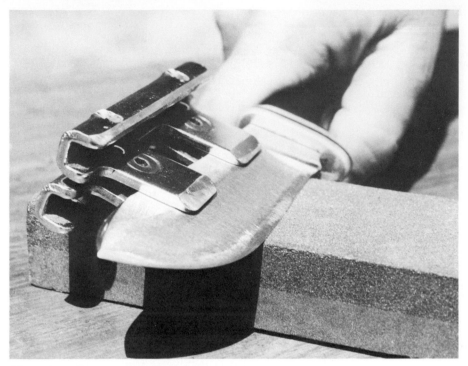

This clamplike device locks onto the blade of a knife and ensures a regular blade-to-stone angle. (Buck Hone-Master)

Once you've achieved a sharp canneled edge, you can work the blade into a coarse grit stone for an even sharper edge and elimination of any rollover. Sharpening steps beyond this aren't necessary, as the impact of chopping will nick a polished edge and quickly return it to a kind of rough-beveled state anyway.

Knives That Won't Take an Edge

Don't forget that there are some knives (usually cheap stainless steel) that simply won't take a good, sharp edge. If you've followed all the sharpening steps correctly and still have a dull knife, chances are you're working with just such a blade. My advice is to throw it out and replace it with a blade of better steel.

There's always the chance, however, that you haven't followed the steps correctly, and, if this is the case, 95 percent of the time you will have failed to hone your initial edge bevel correctly.

PROTECTING AND STORING KNIVES

Knives will dull through use; it's unavoidable. But there are many other sources of dullness and damage that are avoidable.

Outdoor Knife Care

Probably because outdoor knives are burly in appearance, there's the temptation to throw them. Never throw any knife that is not specifically designed for that purpose—which properly limits you to throwing knives.

Some outdoor knives (skin-diving and certain big-game knives) are sturdy enough to classify as utility tools. They have enough steel and strength so that their pommels may be used as hammers and· their blades as light pry bars. These are extremely damaging usages for a knife not designed to take such a beating, so be sure your knife is strong enough before you subject it to this kind of duty.

The most common and avoidable causes of dulling in camping knives are cutting against the ground rather than wood or a board, using the knife to open cans (owing to a lapse of memory and lack of a can opener—we all have had to choose between a sharp knife and starvation at one time or another), and cutting against a tin plate.

Rust and corrosion are the ruination of most fishing knives, and usually result from failure to keep the knife clean and put it away dry.

Hunting knives will chip and nick if you try to chop hard bone, and they'll dull if you try to cut it. They will also stain and rust if you don't keep the blade clean of blood.

When the camping, hunting, or fishing trip is over, wash your knives in warm, soapy water. Use an old toothbrush to clean hard-to-get-to places. Don't leave the knives in the water for a long period of time, and put them away dry.

Pay special attention to leather handles. They are the most susceptible to water damage, and they absorb food residues which make them attractive to gnawing rodents.

Outdoor Knife Storage

Afield, most outdoor knives are carried in a sheath. Skin-diving knives should have plastic sheaths because they're carried underwater,

Sheaths come in a wide variety of styles. The best sheaths have a positive locking device to keep the knife from being lost, and rivets or some other reinforcement at key points where edge and blade work against leather or stitching. Note the two double sheaths at top left; one carries a small sharpening stone, the other a companion caping knife.

One of the most positive knife locks is a peg that fits into the handle, which in turn is held in place by a snap clasp.

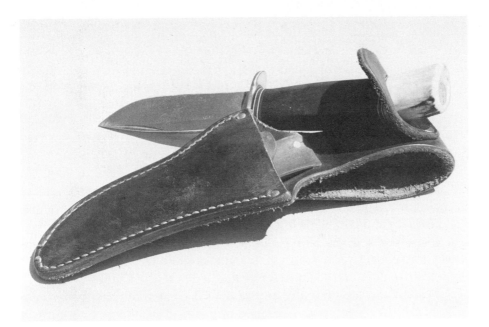

This custom sheath is one of the most foolproof you'll ever find. The blade locks into a plastic insert inside the scabbard, and the handle is encircled by a leather ring. The blade can't work against the leather, and the knife can never fall free.

and survival and service knives often have metal sheaths. Virtually all other knives are carried in leather sheaths.

The function of a sheath is to protect the knife and the carrier. This dictates thick, stiff leather, with rivets or some similar reinforcement in key areas where the edge or point works against stitching. A metal or synthetic cup on the end of the sheath gives extra protection. The point of a knife will eventually pierce the thickest, toughest leather because as you wear the sheath you "work the leather in" and it eventually becomes soft and supple.

Sheaths should lock your knife in place so it can't work free and be lost. The most common locking device is a band of leather that snaps closed around the handle. These can open accidentally, and just such bad luck has cost me two good knives. A full flap that encases the entire knife in a sheath is somewhat safer, as is a peg-and-band clasp. A small peg on the sheath fits into a hole in the knife handle, and a snap clasp around the handle keeps it there.

Never sheath a dirty knife; you will just transfer the dirt to the inside of the scabbard, where elements of corrosion and abrasion can really work on the edge and blade. Although circumstances sometimes dictate otherwise, it's also bad practice to carry a knife in a wet sheath.

When storing an outdoor knife, unsheath the blade and snap the clasp closed around the handle. The salts used to cure leather will corrode the blade if it's left in the sheath for prolonged periods of time. The process is accelerated in humid climates.

Food-Knife Care

Cutting hair, fish scales, and hide is hard on a keen edge, and so is slicing into the soiled skin of unwashed vegetables. Knives can also be dulled by contact with the acids common in tomatoes and citrus fruits and the salts in blood and hot meat. Plain dishwater will also cause a straight carbon blade to pit and corrode along the edge if it's allowed to remain on the knife for protracted periods of time.

Storage and handling practices are even greater culprits than chemicals or the things you cut. The most impractical way to store a knife is in a drawer next to other knives. Edges work against blades as the knives rattle around, and the knives literally unsharpen. And more than once, I've seen knives, steel, and stone stored in the same drawer slot!

This same situation occurs when you wash knives together with plates and silverware. They rattle around against each other and lose their edge. This is particularly harmful in a stainless steel sink. Washing or storing knives together isn't just hard on their edges; it's dangerous too. You're asking for a deep cut as you fish in the dishwater or grope in your knife drawer.

The quickest way to dull a knife is to use it to cut something harder than the steel. When you slice a loaf of bread against a Formica countertop, or cut a steak against a metal serving plate, you're unsharpening the edge. Always use a cutting board, or at least cut against a surface that's markedly softer than the steel in your knife.

Food knives generally have limber or medium-limber spines. Never use these "soft" blades to chop, or their edges to pry, as when separating the hip or leg socket of poultry. This is especially true with a concave or hollow-ground edge.

Don't use tips to pry, either. A knife is a cutting tool, not a screwdriver or a crowbar. Aside from ruining a blade, using a knife to open a painted-closed window or a humidity-swollen drawer is dangerous to you. The blade could slip or splinter.

Dishwashing detergent and hot water will be sufficient to clean most food residues. The safest way to wash a sharp knife is to strop it across a sudsy washcloth, away from the cutting edge. Swish it around in warm water and dry it by stropping. Pay particular attention to the niche where the blade joins the handle or guard. This is a natural place for a buildup of food residues. Clean it with an old toothbrush.

There are some handles that can take a beating from dishwashers and long periods in hot water, but, unless you're sure of its properties, you're better off to hand-wash a knife. Open-pored hardwood handles, or handles with a lot of checkering, deserve a toothbrushing to remove food and the bacteria they may support.

Table knives have an ornamental purpose in addition to their practical one, so a few words on how to keep them looking new and in perfect repair are in order.

Sharpening mistakes will score and scratch a blade, and this will be especially noticeable if it has a mirror polish. You can eliminate all but the deepest scars by buffing the finish on a cloth wheel. These wheels are interchangeable with the stones on a high-speed grinder. Light scratches will be removed by the cloth alone. Deeper scratches will need the abrasive qualities of aluminum oxide powder, the jeweler's rouge.

A neglected carbon blade will rust. If it's deeply pitted, discard the knife—you'll never get down deep enough into the craters of corrosion to keep it clean. Spotty pitting can be ground away with a tool grinder. Light overall rust can be removed by sanding the surface with medium-grit emery cloth.

Both grinders and emery leave relatively deep scars in the metal, so you'll have to do some polishing to guard against future rust. To polish the steel, work the blade over with finer and finer grits of emery. You should get a dull luster after you're done with the finest grit, commonly known as "airplane emery." If you want a mirror polish, you'll have to use a buffing wheel, as described above. You can get a pewter-like polish by rubbing the blade vigorously with fine steel wool. I find this latter finish satisfactory for my purposes; it deters rust and doesn't require the careful attention needed to maintain an unblemished mirror polish.

Rickety handles are usually the result of one of two things: breakage or sprung rivets. If breakage or separation of previously glued parts is repairable, the best glue to use is epoxy. Handles on the more expensive commercial cutlery are often replaceable, so don't overlook the possibility of calling the store where you bought the knife, or writing a short letter to the manufacturer. A really good knife should last you a lifetime, so it's foolish to discard that piece of fine steel for want of a relatively inexpensive handle.

Sprung rivets can usually be made fast again by sandwiching the offending rivet between a surface of hard steel (like an anvil or the back of a vise) and a flat-faced punch of approximately the same diameter as the rivet. Hit the punch once or twice with a hefty hammer, and the rivet should expand into its original firm grip. If the rivet is ruined, you can have the handle reriveted at a machine, motor, or welding shop for under a dollar.

Other parts of certain knives—pommels, guards, spacers and so forth—can be lost or broken. On a quality knife, they're worth repairing, but the technical savvy needed to do so is usually beyond the layman. You can usually get this kind of work done by the manufacturer, or by a jeweler or silversmith.

Kitchen Knife Storage

To maintain a knife's keen edge, you have to prevent it from contacting the steel of another blade. The most practical way to reach this end is rack storage.

The simplest and most convenient knife racks are nothing more than a series of slots cut in a countertop. The blades angle downward and the knife is suspended at the bolster. Stored thus edges and points are protected from accidental contact with your hand and with each other. They're also in full view and easy reach.

If you're short on counter space, a wall rack—a slotted box that can be hung anywhere and that holds between four and six knives—is a practical alternative. It is not quite so convenient as a slotted counter top, however, since getting to the knives usually involves a long reach up or across a counter.

A free-standing knife rack is a slotted box that can be plunked down anywhere. Some of these racks hold knives firmly enough so they can be stored, loaded, on their side in a cabinet or drawer.

opposite: *Knives should be stored carefully. One good way to store kitchen knives is in a slotted counter top.*

Shop-Knife Care

Shop and garden knives are as prone to, and as easily dulled by, drawer storage as food knives. Because these blades are virtually all carbon steel, and because of the nature of their use, they're a lot more likely to rust.

Keep shop knives clean and shiny by frequent buffings or a light once-over with emery, and protect them with a thin coat of machine oil or silicone-based rust retardant like WD-40.

Wooden handles on axes, hatchets, chisels, and drawknives will dry and split with age. You can arrest this process by a once-a-year coating with boiled linseed oil.

Folding knives require more regular cleaning than one-piece knives do. Dirt from your pocket and residues of materials the blade has cut tend to clog up around the bolster and thereby make the blade difficult to open, causing undue wear on moving parts.

If you've used the blade around paint, tar, or certain plant saps, you'll need to first dissolve the buildup with a solvent. I find lighter fluid a capable general-purpose solvent. Next, thoroughly soak the knife in hot, soapy water. Reach the internal recesses with an old toothbrush, and allow the knife to dry with the blades open before returning it to your pocket. If the blades don't open or close smoothly, a drop of oil on the hinges should make them close with a comfortable snap.

Shop-Knife Storage

Some shop tools, like axes, defy storage that's both safe and protective of their edge. For example, hanging an ax on the wall keeps the edge away from dulling contacts—but there's always the remote chance that the ax will fall.

You can make an excellent edge protector for any cutting tool from a length of garden hose or plastic plumbing pipe. Cut a length of tubing 2 inches longer than the edge you want to cover, then slit the hose lengthwise. Nest the edge in the slit. On a sharp-pointed knife, double the end over and secure the bend by whipping it with thread. On a chopping tool like an ax or a cleaver, whip both ends with thread to

opposite: *Another practical method of storing kitchen knives is to keep them in a free-standing knife rack.*

A slit piece of garden hose and strong tape make for excellent edge protection as well as guarding against injuries. This principle may be adapted to virtually any cutting tool.

prevent the hose from sliding forward or backward. The edge protector can be held tightly in place against the blade by either rubber or elastic banding.

Chisels or knives can be stored in the same kind of slotted counter rack that's practical for the kitchen. Another option open is to build a wall rack across the back of your workbench. Just block a strip of 1×2 inch stock ¾ of an inch out from the wall, and you'll have all your tools racked in plain view, showing the dimensions and types of their blades.

A plane should be laid on its side or hung from a pegboard so the blade doesn't bear against any surface. Tools protected by a hose sheath may be stored safely in a drawer.

Index